BEST ⬤ LITTLE
B👁️👁️K
OF BIRDS

Frontispiece: Adult Long-billed Curlew

Published in 2022
by Timber Press, Inc.

The Haseltine Building
133 S.W. Second Avenue, Suite 450
Portland, Oregon 97204-3527
timberpress.com

Printed in China on paper from
responsible resources

Text and cover design by Vincent James

ISBN 978-1-64326-060-0

A catalog record for this book
is available from the Library
of Congress.

BEST LITTLE
BOOK
OF BIRDS

the

OREGON
COAST

Sarah Swanson

TIMBER PRESS

PORTLAND, OREGON

To Max,
Every bird in this book
reminds me of a time
I saw it with you.

CONTENTS

7 Preface

8 Birding the Oregon Coast

24 Bird Family Descriptions

36 Alcids

46 Geese, Ducks & Coots

84 Loons & Grebes

98 Cormorants & Pelicans

106 Oystercatcher & Plovers

116 Sandpipers & Allies

144 Herons & Egrets

148 Shearwaters, Gulls & Terns

166 Vultures, Osprey, Hawks, Eagles & Falcons

182 Pigeons

184 Kingfishers

186 Woodpeckers

192 Jays, Crows & Ravens

198 Hummingbirds

202 Swallows

212 Chickadees & Wrentit

218 Kinglets & Vireos

224 Flycatchers

228 Wrens

234 Thrushes & Waxwings

242 Finches

250 Sparrows

264 Blackbirds

270 Warblers

282 Tanagers & Grosbeaks

286 Accessible Birding Sites

287 Recommended Resources

288 Acknowledgments

289 Photo and Illustration Credits

292 Bibliography

294 Index

Preface

As a young birder, I gazed through my clunky old binoculars at the colorful Northern Flickers and busy Bushtits in my Portland neighborhood, relishing the feeling of discovery. I watched my first Vaux's Swifts flutter over my elementary school and fell in love with the antics of American Dippers on a fishing trip with my grandfather. Soon, though, I was ready for the broader birding horizons that I found at the Oregon Coast when my family visited each summer. Noisy Caspian Terns roosted on a sand spit, and a Green Heron waded in the shallows of the marina where we bought crab bait. Pigeon Guillemots paddled with red feet below the docks in Newport, and pushy Western Gulls waited impatiently for dropped food. Once, I locked eyes with a Wrentit peering out of the dense brush along a Cape Perpetua trail. The coast offered exciting birding encounters everywhere I looked—the abundance and variety took my interest in birding to a new level.

But finding these new birds in my field guide wasn't always easy—there were so many birds to flip through, and sometimes I would think I'd figured one out, only to see that that particular bird wasn't found nearby. When the opportunity to write a bird book focused on the Oregon Coast came along, I was excited to provide a better option for those exploring the region's birds. I hope that this field guide will spark interest in the coast's fascinating bird fauna, simplify identification, and inspire birders to learn more about the challenges facing many coastal birds and the ways that we can help them.

Birding
the Oregon Coast

The raucous sound of nesting seabirds hits you first, followed closely by the fishy smell. As you walk the short trail past the Yaquina Head Lighthouse, a large flat-topped rock just offshore comes into view. Common Murres are packed together, constantly jostling and screaming at one another. Birds land in a steady stream carrying fish for their fluffy nestlings as others depart to forage. On the cliff below you, a Brandt's Cormorant flutters its bright blue throat patch to impress its mate. You set up your spotting scope and a quick scan of the ocean reveals a flock of Surf Scoters with their telltale bright bills. Another pass reveals a chunky Rhinoceros Auklet floating at the edge of a flock of murres. Scoping the intertidal area, you see a Black Oystercatcher pecking at a mussel bed while a small group of Harlequin Ducks roosts nearby, looking like a cluster of round rocks. The longer you stand there, the more you see. A line of Brown Pelicans flies by, shadowed by pale-headed Heermann's Gulls. Looking for lunch, a Peregrine Falcon rides the wind on pointed wings.

The appeal of the Oregon Coast as a birding destination is a combination of its natural beauty, the diverse habitats that are home to a

A Common Murre lands at its breeding colony with a fish.

wide array of bird species, and the expanses of public land that provide abundant access to excellent birding sites.

Seasonal pulses of migrants fill trees with songbirds, cover bays with ducks, and pepper beaches with busily foraging sandpipers. Shorebird and songbird migrations begin each spring, and breeding songbirds and seabirds stay at the Oregon Coast all summer. Their southward migration begins in late summer, and then the cast of coastal bird species changes again. Fall brings waterfowl, sparrows, and raptors to the coast, where they brave rain and storms all winter. Migrating birds connect the Oregon Coast to distant parts of the world, from the arctic tundra breeding grounds of sandpipers, to the verdant tropical rainforests where warblers winter, to the remote South Pacific breeding islands of shearwaters.

Finding a place to enjoy coastal birds couldn't be easier. There are more than 75 state-run parks, recreation sites, scenic viewpoints, waysides, and natural areas along the coast. Many of these sites are small, but offer a view of the ocean or access to the beach. Larger parks also provide picnic areas, hiking, and camping. Federally managed public lands along the coast include wildlife refuges, forests, and the Oregon Dunes Recreation Area. The Oregon Beach Bill guarantees public access to Oregon's 363 miles of beaches, so there is a lot of room to explore.

Coastal Habitats

The stunning vistas of the Oregon Coast are made up of a combination of sedimentary rocks like sandstone, that erode more quickly, and volcanic rocks like basalt, that can withstand the ocean's weathering. Lava flows and eruptions have created dramatic headlands and small, rocky offshore islands that are home to many species of birds. Water interacts with the coastal geology to create a variety of habitats.

Wet, stormy winters and springs at the coast give way to drier summers. It rarely freezes along the coast, leaving lots of open water for birds. The South Coast is even warmer, and the "banana belt" around Brookings can reach 70 degrees in the winter. The Coast Range, mountains that run north–south between the coast and Oregon's interior valleys, gets even more rain than the coast itself, with some places receiving over 120 inches per year. This huge amount of water is channeled into the many rivers flowing out of the Coast Range, forming bays and estuaries on their way to the ocean.

The original stewards of this land and its birds were the many indigenous peoples of the region who shaped this landscape and who still reside on the land. Conservation efforts that return land to coastal tribes can play an important role in both ecological and cultural restoration.

BAYS AND ESTUARIES

Bays are created where a river has a gently sloping path to the sea and room to spread out. Bays have saltwater areas near their mouths, freshwater areas where rivers come in, and estuaries in between. Estuaries are where fresh and saltwater meet and mix. These nutrient-rich areas are home to a rich food web of plankton, worms, fish, crabs, and other creatures. The estuarine mudflats revealed at low tide may seem barren, but shorebirds like plovers, sandpipers, godwits, and dowitchers have bills that are perfect tools for extracting hidden worms and clams. Beds of eelgrass in estuaries provide food for migrating and wintering Brants. When the seas get rough in winter, bays provide a calm refuge for scoters, loons, and grebes.

Iconic bay birds include Black-bellied Plover, Brant, and Caspian Tern. Find them at South Slough National Estuarine Research Reserve, Bandon Marsh National Wildlife Refuge, Bayocean Peninsula, and the Mark Hatfield Marine Science Center and Estuary Trail.

Birding tips: At low tide, exposed mudflats are wide; shorebirds are feeding, but may be far from view. Birding on the incoming tide allows the advancing water to crowd the birds together and push them toward you. Use extreme care not to get stuck when exploring mudflats.

ROCKY SHORES AND ISLANDS

Basalt and sandstone outcroppings provide an anchoring place for a rich variety of marine organisms like limpets and mussels that in turn are food for birds. The twice-daily cycles of the tide obscure and reveal the intertidal area, closing and opening the buffet. Tall rocky cliffs and islands also provide nesting sites for seabirds. Jetties are fingers of rock constructed at the mouths of rivers to provide safe passage for boats through the waves, but they also provide additional rocky habitat.

Iconic rocky shore birds include Black Oystercatcher, Harlequin Duck, Surfbird, and Black Turnstone. Find them at Yaquina Head Outstanding Natural Area, Haystack Rock at Cannon Beach, and Cape Arago State Park.

Birding tips: At high tide, birds on rocks are more concentrated but will likely be roosting and may have their heads tucked. Low tide

A group of Black Oystercatchers roosts near the surf.

exposes more foraging habitat, and birds are more active. Avoid trampling sensitive intertidal habitat or disturbing nesting birds.

SANDY BEACHES AND DUNES

Beaches provide foraging opportunities for many birds and nesting sites for a few specialized ones. Food items like tiny shrimp are constantly being washed in by the waves, and retreating water exposes worms and other creatures burying themselves in the sand. Mole crabs in particular are food for whimbrels and godwits that probe the sand with their long bills for these crunchy little nuggets. Each high tide leaves a wrack line of debris that attracts amphipods, also known as sand fleas, a favorite food of birds. On the dry sand, shells and sticks camouflage the nests of wary plovers.

Iconic sandy beach birds include Snowy Plover, Whimbrel, and Sanderling. Find them at Nehalem Bay State Park, Fort Stevens State Park, and Oregon Dunes Recreation Area.

Birding tips: Spring and fall migration are the best times to see shorebirds on the beach. You may need to cover some ground and spend a while walking the beach to find them. There are also a few places in Oregon where driving on the beach is allowed. This provides access for those with mobility issues, but it's important to drive slowly and disturb birds as little as possible.

OCEAN

Shallow nearshore ocean areas provide foraging grounds for diving birds like sea ducks and alcids, while albatrosses and shearwaters cruise over the deeper pelagic zone and offshore canyons. The array of birds visible from shore varies with the seasons, as murres and puffins come to shore to breed in summer, and loons, grebes, and scoters float the seas in winter.

Iconic oceangoing birds include Marbled Murrelet, White-winged Scoter, and Pacific Loon. Find them at Seaside Cove, Boiler Bay State Scenic Viewpoint, and Chetco Point Park.

Birding tips: For a good view of birds on the ocean, you need a viewpoint that is both close to the ocean and high enough to let you see over the waves. Some birds will be close enough to view with binoculars, but seawatching is much more satisfying with a spotting scope that will resolve those distant specks into identifiable birds. For an adventure and a chance to see birds that live beyond the sight of land, take a pelagic birding trip by boat.

FORESTS

Forests along the coast vary from primeval, moss-covered Sitka spruce and cedar in the north to myrtle, redwood, and rhododendron in the south. Shore pine thrives in sandy and exposed areas, and alder and maple grow in previously logged areas and along rivers. Forests provide nesting and foraging habitat for a large number of songbirds, woodpeckers, raptors, and owls.

Iconic birds of coastal forests include Hermit Warbler, Swainson's Thrush, and Pacific Wren. Find them at Ecola State Park, Cape Perpetua, and Humbug Mountain State Park.

Birding tips: Forest birding is at its best in spring when migrant songbirds arrive. Because birds are often high in trees and obscured by leaves, birding by ear is important. To get a better view of canopy-dwelling birds, find an opening in the forest, like a parking lot, where you can see up into the tops of the trees. In winter listen for the high chatter of chickadees and kinglets to find mixed-species flocks of birds foraging together.

COASTAL PRAIRIES AND FIELDS

Open areas are great places to watch birds of prey. True coastal prairies are rare today because of human use and the proliferation of exotic plant species. Pastures and agricultural fields are more common, especially on the flatter North Coast. Many birds, both native and introduced, make their homes around farms because of the food resources like grain, rodents, and insects that are available there.

Iconic birds of coastal fields include Great Egret, Black Phoebe, and Red-shouldered Hawk. Find them at Wireless Road near Astoria, Tillamook River Wetlands, and Nestucca Bay National Wildlife Refuge.

Birding tips: Scan fence lines for songbirds like phoebes and sparrows. Check the tops of trees along the edge of fields for raptors. The edges of pastures often have brambles, bushes, and weeds that are home to sparrows.

FRESHWATER WETLANDS

Freshwater wetlands and marshes are not unique to the coast, but they are great places to find birds. Plants like grasses, sedges, cattails, and willows provide cover and nesting sites, and aquatic insects and plant seeds are food for a variety of bird species. Wetlands are home to waterfowl, raptors, shorebirds, herons, and songbirds. Sewage and settling ponds provide a surrogate for wetlands where they are uncommon and can be excellent birding locations.

Iconic wetland birds include Common Yellowthroat, Marsh Wren, and Northern Harrier. Find them at Cannon Beach Settling Ponds, Tillamook River Wetlands, Millicoma Marsh, and Bandon Marsh National Wildlife Refuge.

Birding tips: Listen for the songs and calls of birds to alert you to their presence in the tall grass. Scan open areas for shorebirds like Least Sandpiper and Killdeer. Sewage ponds vary widely in the level of access that they offer: some have public trails, some are completely off limits, and others require you to obtain a permit or permission. Research before you go.

Coastal Conservation Issues

Birds at the coast face both universal threats and unique challenges. Climate change threatens coastal birds in multiple ways. Rising seas are a danger to birds like Black Oystercatchers that nest and forage in a narrow area around the intertidal zone. Warming ocean temperatures cause declines in the populations of small fish like anchovies that Brown Pelicans and many other seabirds eat. Ocean acidification threatens shellfish and the scoters, turnstones, and oystercatchers that eat them.

Habitat destruction affects many coastal birds, but it is especially critical in the case of the endangered Marbled Murrelet. Murrelets nest on the mossy limbs of large, old trees within 50 miles of the coast, commuting daily to the ocean. Preservation of the small amount of coastal old-growth forest that has not yet been logged is critical to the survival of this unique species.

Fishing at the beach is popular with both birds and humans, but only humans leave fishing line behind. Fishing line entanglement kills many coastal birds, especially murres, gulls, cormorants, and ducks. This problem is much easier to fix than some of the others that face birds. When fishing, always gather up stray fishing line and put it in an appropriate receptacle. If you find any fishing line or lures when birding, take them with you.

Another direct threat that people pose to coastal birds is the disturbance of nesting and roosting sites. Approaching nesting areas, especially with dogs, can easily disturb birds like Snowy Plovers and Black Oystercatchers. Flushing a nesting bird exposes the eggs and chicks to predation. Roosting birds need rest to conserve energy, especially during migration.

Though it may seem like the deck is stacked against coastal birds, there are still many things that we can do to help as individuals and communities.

How to Help Coastal Birds

SUPPORT the formation of Marine Protected Areas that provide refuge to ocean fish and increase their populations.

ADVOCATE for the protection of remaining areas of old-growth forest.

REDUCE your carbon emissions from fossil fuels and ask the same of corporations and governments.

CHOOSE ocean-friendly options when you eat seafood. See seafoodwatch.org.

OBEY nesting-season closures and restrictions. Enjoy birds from a respectful distance.

PICK UP stray fishing line and dispose of it properly.

JOIN one of several volunteer community science projects that monitor coastal bird species. Contact Portland Audubon for more information: audubonportland.org.

TRAIN to become a Coastal Observation and Seabird Survey Team (COASST) volunteer, and monitor beaches for beached birds.

REPORT banded plovers: See a Snowy Plover during the fall or winter? Take a photo or write down the color band pattern and report it to reportband.gov

A Marbled Murrelet sits on its nest on a mossy branch, high in the forest.

Gear and Safety

There are no hard rules about birding gear, and you can enjoy birds without any financial investment. That said, a pair of waterproof binoculars will go a long way toward improving your birding experience. If you want to spend a lot of time birding at the coast, a spotting scope (also waterproof) is ideal for better views of birds seen out on the ocean or far down a beach. A scope increases your magnification from the 8x of typical binoculars to 20x–60x. A camera can also be useful for documenting rarities or challenging identifications, and you can even take photos with your phone through binoculars or a scope. Recording your sightings can be done with a smartphone app like eBird or in a notebook. Finally, remember that there is no bad weather, only inadequate rain gear.

In some ways the Oregon Coast is a benign place: the weather is rarely hot or below freezing, and there are no venomous snakes. The ocean, however, requires vigilance. Birders should be wary of both incoming tides and unpredictably large "sneaker waves" that can crash over rocks and rush shockingly far up the beach. Large waves can also crash over jetties and shift rocks and logs. A good rule of thumb is to never turn

A pair of
Harlequin
Ducks

your back on the ocean or take your eyes off it for too long. Other coastal hazards include crumbling cliffs, and mudflats where it is easy to get stuck when water levels come up quickly on incoming tides. Birders should always be aware of their environment and possible hazards. Check tidesandcurrents.noaa.gov for tidal predictions and weather.gov for warnings about large waves and hazardous weather.

Accessibility

Birding is for everyone. You don't have to climb a mountain or hike through soft sand to get a great view of birds on the Oregon Coast. Birders with mobility challenges will find trails and viewpoints that offer access to a variety of habitats. The Oregon State Parks website has information about and photos of accessible features at each park to allow visitors to find parks that work for them. Seaside, Cannon Beach, and Manzanita all offer special wheelchairs for visitors to use on the beach. A list of some recommended accessible birding sites can be found in the back of this book. See birdability.org for more information about removing barriers for birders.

Adult Peregrine Falcon

Birding Ethics

EBIRD BASICS

eBird is a website (ebird.org) and smartphone app from Cornell Lab of Ornithology. It is a valuable tool for birders and has many functions:

- Track your sightings and generate customizable lists
- Contribute to a scientific database
- Find birds and birding hotspots
- Get customized alerts for rare birds and target species

It is important to make the well-being of birds a priority, even if it means not getting the best view or photograph. Watch birds for signs that they are disturbed by your presence, and back off if necessary. Be especially sensitive around nesting sites.

As a person in public with binoculars, you are an ambassador of the birding community. Be kind to other birders and stay out of private property and closed areas of parks and refuges. The American Birding Association (ABA) details a complete Code of Birding Ethics at americanbirding.org.

A flock of Snowy Plovers takes flight on a busy beach.

Bird Names for Birds

Bird names can highlight distinctive plumage, geographical range, song, or habitat, and provide helpful information. Many birds, however, are named after people, including the Townsend's Warbler, Heermann's Gull, and Steller's Jay in this book. The #BirdNamesForBirds campaign wants to change the bird names that honor people because these names were applied by European and American naturalists as part of colonialism and are, therefore, associated with racism and exploitation. New names could make the birding community more welcoming and equitable. The discussion in the birding and ornithology communities on this subject is ongoing, but the American Ornithological Society, in charge of bird names, is looking into how to address the issue.

Using this Book

This book focuses on the 124 birds that are most likely to be found on the Oregon Coast. Less common birds are also mentioned but do not have their own entries. The classification system used by scientists worldwide categorizes living things into smaller and smaller related groups, the last three being family, genus, and species. In this section you will find an introduction to the families featured in the book and learn what characteristics exemplify the members of each. Individual bird entries will include its genus and species. In a departure from the typical field guide format that groups birds solely by genetic relationships, this book groups bird families that are genetically unrelated but resemble each other and share the same habitat. For example, the unrelated guillemots, scoters, grebes, and loons that you might see swimming near each other in a bay have been placed on adjacent pages for easier comparison.

Each species entry provides the following specifics:

PHOTOS
of the plumages most likely to be seen on the Oregon Coast.

CAPTIONS
detailing key field marks.

HABITAT AND BEHAVIOR Which habitats the bird prefers on the Oregon Coast, what it eats, nesting behavior if it breeds at the coast, and any other distinctive behaviors.

YEARLY ABUNDANCE When and where to find the bird and how common it is at the Oregon Coast. These categories are not indicators of absolute abundance but provide an idea of how likely you are to find each species during the months indicated. Sites listed are by no means the only places that the birds can be found, but they represent the type of habitat where you are likely to see them, and they are all great birding spots.

> **RARE** | It would be exciting to see this bird because it doesn't happen very often.
> **UNCOMMON** | You might see this bird, especially in the right habitat.
> **COMMON** | You will see this bird most of the time.
> **VERY COMMON** | It would be hard not to find this bird.

SOUNDS The various songs (complex sounds often used for territorial and courtship purposes) and calls (short sounds used as alarms or for communication within flocks) made during the time this bird is at the coast. Breeding season sounds are not included for birds that only spend the winter in Oregon.

SIMILAR SPECIES Birds with similar shape or plumage that could be confused for the featured species. Less common birds may only be shown on the page of a similar, more common species.

SIZE OF THE BIRD in length (head to tail) and wingspan.

Bird Family Descriptions

A "family" is a group of closely related species that share physical characteristics and behaviors. Each family has a name in English and one in Latin, the language of scientific classification. Learning to recognize a bird family can help you narrow down the possible species when you are trying to identify an unfamiliar bird.

ALCIDS (family Alcidae)

Alcids are awkward on land, waddling with legs positioned near the back of their stubby bodies. They also seem labored in flight, but are completely at ease underwater where they use their wings to "fly" gracefully after fish. Alcids are primarily oceanic, with some venturing into bays.

GEESE & DUCKS (family Anatidae)

Waterfowl have adaptations for a life lived in and around the water, including webbed feet and waterproof plumage. Their bills fit their foraging methods: serrated bills for grabbing fish, thick bills for crushing mollusks, or comblike "teeth" for filtering out small invertebrates. Most waterfowl visit the Oregon Coast only during migration and over the winter when they sport bright, fresh plumage.

COOTS (family Rallidae)

Coots are loud and gregarious, diving and squabbling in open water. Their feet have fleshy pads, or lobes, that help them swim but also spread out their weight when they walk on mud or floating plants. Though they may resemble ducks in shape and behavior, they are actually related to rails, which are secretive wetland dwellers.

LOONS (family Gaviidae)

Loons have sharp, pointed bills that help them to grab fish, and webbed feet placed at the very back of their bodies to make swimming more efficient. Loons breed in northern areas but spend the winter on the coast. Young birds may also remain along the coast in summer. During spring and fall migration, large numbers of loons can be seen flying over the ocean with their long necks drooping.

GREBES (family Podicipedidae)

Grebes are adapted to a life lived on the water. They swim underwater to catch food, propelled by lobed feet set at the back of their bodies. Grebes have dense bones that make it easier for them to stay underwater, and they can decrease their buoyancy by holding their feathers more closely to their bodies. Most grebes at the coast are there only for the winter.

CORMORANTS (family Phalacrocoracidae)

Cormorants propel themselves underwater with webbed feet and grab fish with hooked bills. They can often be seen holding their wings open while roosting in order to dry their feathers and regulate their body temperature. Three cormorant species breed on the Oregon Coast, each with its own nesting niche.

PELICANS (family Pelecanidae)

Pelicans are instantly recognizable by their huge, pouched bills. These pouches are used to grab large volumes of water and small fish. The water is then drained and the fish swallowed. Pelicans also have large, webbed feet to help them paddle. Their long, broad wings allow them to soar in flocks or glide over the waves with ease.

OYSTERCATCHERS
(family Haematopodidae)

These large, odd-looking shorebirds are unsurprisingly in a separate family from plovers and sandpipers. Black Oystercatchers are larger and heavier than most shorebirds, with a laterally flattened bill that is specially adapted to pry limpets and mussels from intertidal rocks. These foods are available year-round and so are oystercatchers, remaining in the vicinity of their nesting sites all winter.

PLOVERS (family Charadriidae)

Plovers occupy similar habitat to sandpipers and look superficially similar, but plovers have rounder bodies, shorter bills, and large eyes. They are visual predators that catch invertebrates by running around and jabbing their bills into mud or sand in open areas.

SANDPIPERS (family Scolopacidae)

Sandpipers are outfitted with bills in an array of shapes and sizes that allow them to forage in rocky shores, sandy beaches, estuarine mudflats, freshwater wetlands, and the open ocean. Many sandpipers only pass through Oregon on migrations between their southern wintering grounds and their breeding grounds on the northern tundra. This creates a surge of shorebirds on our shores in April–May and July–September.

HERONS & EGRETS (family Ardeidae)

Herons and egrets have long necks, long pointed bills, and long legs that allow them to wade when hunting for food. They are found in and around water, including bays, rivers, and wetlands, but they also hunt in fields for frogs, small mammals, and snakes. The mild winter temperatures and abundant food in bays and estuaries make the coast an important refuge for these birds.

SHEARWATERS (family Procellariidae)

Shearwaters are part of a group known as tubenoses. They glide long distances over the ocean on long, thin wings, coming to land only to nest. Tubelike nostrils on their bills allow them to drip out extra salt from drinking seawater. They also sniff out concentrations of plankton while on the wing. Only the Sooty Shearwater is easily seen from shore in Oregon, while other tubenoses are seen in the pelagic zone farther offshore.

GULLS & TERNS (family Laridae)

Gulls and terns both have webbed feet and an affinity for water, but terns dive headfirst for fish and have long pointed wings and sharply pointed bills, and gulls have blunter bills and larger feet for swimming and walking. Gulls can be a challenge to identify because their plumage varies with age and season, and they hybridize with each other. Despite these complexities, gulls have key field marks that allow many of them to be confidently named.

VULTURES (family Cathartidae)

Only one species of vulture can currently be found in Oregon. Historically, California Condors also roamed Oregon's coastline, but their range has been drastically reduced as a result of their near extinction. Vultures serve a vital role in the ecosystem by eating dead animals and thereby preventing the spread of disease. Their bald heads are an adaptation to eating carrion: a featherless head is much easier to clean after being stuck inside a seal carcass.

OSPREY (family Pandionidae)
HAWKS & EAGLES (family Accipitridae)

Osprey, hawks, and eagles are known as diurnal raptors, meaning that they hunt during the day. Their adaptations for hunting include sharp talons, strong feet, and acute eyesight and hearing. Many raptors are more prevalent on the coast in the winter, visiting because the temperate climate and lack of snow cover make rodents available year-round.

FALCONS (family Falconidae)

Falcons are birds of prey but are not closely related to hawks and eagles. Notable adaptations include a notched bill for severing their prey's spine and a bony bump in their nostril that allows them to breathe while diving at high speeds. Falcons can be differentiated from hawks at a distance by their "hunched" shoulders, relatively short bill, and long pointed wings.

PIGEONS & DOVES (family Columbidae)

Pigeons and doves are easily recognized by their small heads and plump bodies and have unique behaviors that facilitate their plant-based diets. Doves consume small pieces of gravel along roads to help their muscular gizzards digest hard seeds. Berry-eating pigeons need minerals found in certain clay soil and fly long distances to visit sites where it is available.

KINGFISHERS (family Alcedinidae)

Kingfishers have long, heron-like bills that help them to pluck fish from the water. They are one of a small number of Oregon birds that excavate burrows, an impressive task to accomplish using only a bill. The coast is an ideal place for kingfishers with its abundance of watery habitats that rarely freeze over.

WOODPECKERS (family Picidae)

Woodpeckers are quickly recognized by their vertical perching and their hammering on trees. They have several adaptations to their arboreal, insectivorous lifestyle, including long tongues, chisel-like bills, stiff tail feathers that brace them as they cling to trees, and specialized skulls that cushion their brains. Detecting woodpeckers is easiest in spring when they are loudly calling, drumming, and excavating.

JAYS, CROWS & RAVENS
(family Corvidae)

Corvids are known for their intelligence and good memories, and these omnivorous birds take advantage of the foraging opportunities presented by human activity. Though they might not be what you think of when you think about songbirds, corvids are talented vocalists, capable of a wide variety of calls for social communication and mimicry.

HUMMINGBIRDS (family Trochilidae)

Hummingbirds are immediately recognizable by their tiny size, hovering flight, and needlelike bills. Their wings move in a figure eight motion, faster than our eyes can see, which allows them to hover and fly both forward and backward. The mild winters and early springs of the Oregon Coast suit hummingbirds well, and the area is home to both a resident species and a migratory breeder.

SWALLOWS (family Hirundinidae)

Swallows specialize in eating aerial insects on the wing. They have long, pointed wings for acrobatic flight and gaping mouths to catch their prey, and they can be found around high concentrations of flying insects: over fields, wetlands, and sewage ponds. These long-distance migrants breed in Oregon and gather in large mixed-species flocks to migrate south for the winter.

CHICKADEES (family Paridae)

The Oregon Coast has two chickadee species that can be seen year-round. Their vocal nature and constant activity make chickadees easy to find, though Chestnut-backed Chickadees are often higher up in trees. A loud, long series of chickadee alarm calls is worth following because it may indicate the presence of an owl or other predator.

WRENTIT (family Sylviidae)

The Wrentit is a taxonomic oddball, having landed in its current family after much taxonomic shuffling. It is the only local representative of a bird family otherwise found in Eurasia and Africa.

KINGLETS (family Regulidae)

Kinglets are small insectivorous birds with brightly colored crests. Their more evocatively named Old World relatives include Goldcrests, Flamecrests, and Firecrests. Both kinglets in Oregon have very active feeding behavior, but the two vary in habitat, migration pattern, and vocalizations.

VIREOS (family Vireonidae)

Vireos occupy a similar niche to that of warblers as insectivorous foliage gleaners, but they are larger with hooked bills. They hover less than warblers and can be more difficult to spot because of it. They are known for their frequent singing, often continuing to sing all day long.

FLYCATCHERS (family Tyrannidae)

Flycatchers share an upright posture, large squarish heads, and the behavior for which they are named: sighting flying invertebrates from a perch and flying out to grab them. Many flycatchers are neotropical migrants and spend the winter in Central America. Black Phoebes are the only resident flycatcher on the Oregon Coast, enjoying the mild winters and the invertebrates found around dairy farms and sewage treatment ponds.

WRENS (family Troglodytidae)

Troglodytidae means "cave dweller," alluding to the way that wrens creep into cracks and crevices in search of food. They are often found near the ground where they forage for insects with their long bills. Wrens occur year-round at the Oregon Coast and make themselves heard in habitats from old-growth forests to wetlands.

THRUSHES (family Turdidae)

Thrushes are rounded, upright songbirds that have relatively large eyes to help them spot prey on the ground. A specialized vocal organ called the syrinx allows them to sing beautiful, polyphonic songs—singing multiple notes at once. Thrushes occupy several habitat types and have varied migratory strategies, so there is almost always one to enjoy.

WAXWINGS (family Bombycillidae)

There are only three species of waxwings on earth, including the Cedar Waxwing, a familiar sight on berry bushes in Oregon. Waxwings rely so heavily on berries that they breed later in the summer than most birds to ensure a supply of ripe fruits to feed their young. Waxwings move around to take advantage of seasonal berry availability, and their presence can be unpredictable outside of the breeding season.

FINCHES (family Fringillidae)

Finches have a primarily vegetarian diet and even feed seeds to their young. Many species are irruptive, moving around in large numbers to follow high seed abundance. Their seed-eating habit also makes finches reliable backyard feeder birds. Finches are noisy, singing and calling frequently, which helps in locating and identifying them.

SPARROWS (family Passerellidae)

The small, brown birds in this family have a reputation for being difficult to identify, sometimes dismissed as "little brown jobs." Their heads and underparts, however, have distinctive plumage that makes identification mostly straightforward. Sparrows often hide in grass and bushes but are responsive to being lured into the open by "pishing," squeaking and smacking with your mouth to mimic bird alarm calls.

BLACKBIRDS (family Icteridae)

Blackbirds are a vocal group of birds whose plumage colors often include yellow and red in addition to the expected black. Birds in this family have relatively long legs and easily walk on the ground. Most have pointed bills for grabbing insects. Blackbirds and cowbirds form multispecies flocks in the winter and are found around farms where they can feed on spilled grain.

WARBLERS (family Parulidae)

Warblers are small birds that catch insects and other arthropods with their thin, pointed bills. Most warblers are shades of yellow, though there are exceptions to any rule about birds. Each species has a distinctive song and chip call that can be identified. Migration season (April and May) is the best time to find warblers because they pass through in large numbers, are actively foraging all day to refuel, and are less picky about habitat.

TANAGERS & GROSBEAKS

(family Cardinalidae)

This group of colorful birds only has a few representatives along the Oregon Coast, but you won't want to miss them. As befitting their membership in a family full of tropical birds, tanagers and grosbeaks of the Oregon Coast are bright and beautiful. They spend the winter in Mexico and Central America, then appear in Oregon as spring is taking hold. They have larger bills than warblers, eating fruit and large insects.

Breeding adult.
Looks bulky, with a
long, pointed bill. Black
above and white below.

Breeding adult.
Upright posture on land.
Solid brownish black hood.

Nonbreeding adult.
White chin and collar with a black
cap and black streak behind the eye.

COMMON MURRE

Uria aalge

These colonial seabirds bring noise and excitement to rocky islands when they return each spring. Oregon's largest alcids are great fathers, feeding their chicks after they leave the nest and jump into the sea.

Feeds on small fish, crustaceans, and mollusks in bays and in the ocean. Nests in loud, crowded colonies on off-shore rocks and seaside cliffs. Does not construct a nest, but lays an egg on bare rock.

Look for them nesting at Three Arch Rocks National Wildlife Refuge viewed from Oceanside, Yaquina Head Outstanding Natural Area, and Coquille Point. Common during the breeding season and uncommon in winter.

Vocal at the nest, where they bark, groan, and screech.

Similar species: see Pigeon Guillemot entry page 39 and Marbled Murrelet entry page 41.

Breeding adult.
Distinctive white wing
patches and red feet.

Breeding adult.
Body and head are
black. Mouth is red.

Nonbreeding adult.
Grayish head, white underparts, and
a mottled black-and-white back.

PIGEON GUILLEMOT

Cephhus columba

Their distinctive plumage and habit of hanging out in calm bays make them the perfect introduction to seabirds. Nest boxes under the docks in Yaquina Bay provide homes for a boisterous colony of guillemots.

Nests in caves and crevices and under docks. Diet consists primarily of small bottom-dwelling fish. Feeds in bays and the ocean and is more likely to be seen in bays than other alcids. Courtship behavior includes underwater chasing and the rubbing together of bills.

Look for them at Haystack Rock near Cannon Beach, in Yaquina Bay, and at Harris Beach State Park. Common March–August.

Song is an accelerating series of shrill "pseeps." Call is a whistled "seer."

Similar species: see Common Murre entry page 37 and nonbreeding Marbled Murrelet entry page 41.

Breeding adult.
Marbled dark brown all over. Bill is thin, pointed, and dark.

Nonbreeding adult.
White throat and collar and a black cap over the eye.

Nonbreeding or juvenile Ancient Murrelet.
Head has more extensive black. Back is gray.

MARBLED MURRELET

Brachyramphus marmoratus

These small seabirds live at the intersection of two iconic Pacific Northwest habitats: old-growth forest and ocean. Changes in both of these habitats have caused murrelets to be listed as threatened under the federal Endangered Species Act and endangered by the State of Oregon.

Spends the winter at sea. Feeds on a variety of small fish caught by swimming underwater near shore. Nests in older forests with large, old conifers. Lays one egg on a large moss-covered branch of a conifer tree many miles from the ocean.

Look for them from raised viewpoints near Cape Perpetua, at Cape Arago State Park, and Chetco Point Park. Uncommon year-round.

Gives a high "keer" and sometimes a nasal "mew" as it flies through the forest around dusk and dawn, traveling back and forth from its nest.

Ancient Murrelet is rare November–January.

Breeding adult. Thin white plumes on the face, and a small, white horn on the bill.

Nonbreeding adult. Dark gray plumage with a paler belly visible in flight. Bill is thick and dark yellow-orange.

RHINOCEROS AUKLET

Cerorhinca monocerata

Though they are often overshadowed by the more brightly colored puffins, these seabirds with their namesake horns are worth searching for. Rhinoceros Auklets typically only visit their nests at night, but they can be seen visiting nests inside Sea Lion Caves during the day.

Seen on the ocean near shore. Nests in small numbers along the Oregon Coast in burrows on rocky islands or in caves. Dives to catch fish and load up its bill to feed nestlings.

Look for them on the water from Barview Jetty, Yaquina Head Outstanding Natural Area, and Cape Arago State Park. Rare in winter and uncommon otherwise.

Makes moans and grunts in the nest burrow.

Similar species: see Tufted Puffin entry page 45.

Breeding adult.
Face is white with thick pale yellow plumes. Bill is large and bright orange with a dull yellow base. Feet are orange.

Adults at a burrow.

TUFTED PUFFIN

Fratercula cirrhata

A large, chunky alcid that flies around offshore rocks looking like a black football wearing a clown mask. Its annual return to coastal nesting sites is eagerly awaited by puffin enthusiasts.

Seen on the ocean or flying around near nesting areas. Nests in burrows on rocky islands and can sometimes be spotted near the burrow entrance. Both parents bring bills full of fish and squid to the pufflings.

Look for them at Haystack Rock near Cannon Beach for the closest views and also at Face Rock Wayside and Harris Beach State Park. Present on their breeding grounds April–September but move far out to sea in winter.

Not usually heard. Makes a low moan in the nest burrow.

Similar species: see Rhinoceros Auklet entry page 43.

Adult.
Black goose with a white collar
and dark belly. More white on
the tail than other geese.

BRANT

Branta bernicla

This well-dressed goose visits estuaries to feast on eelgrass, which it folds up with its tongue before swallowing. Found in flocks numbering into the hundreds during migration.

Found on estuarine mudflats and in bays. Sometimes seen resting on beaches. Diet is specialized, consisting primarily of eelgrass and some green algae. Easily disturbed by recreation and aquaculture activities on eelgrass beds.

Look for them at Bayocean Peninsula, Mark Hatfield Marine Science Center and Estuary Trail, and Charleston Boat Basin. Rare to uncommon October–May.

Makes a low honk and bleat. Not as noisy as other geese, but birds in flocks chatter to each other.

Similar species: see Cackling Goose entry page 49.

Adult.
White cheeks, stubby bill, steep forehead, and short neck. Breast color varies from gray to purplish brown. Some have a white ring at the base of the neck.

CACKLING GOOSE

Branta hutchinsii

This petite cousin of the well-known Canada Goose is smaller in every way but its migrations. The subpopulation of Semidi Island Aleutian Cackling Geese migrates from its breeding site in Alaska to winter in farm fields around Pacific City, Oregon. Each night, geese fly out from the fields to roost on or around Haystack Rock.

Found in pastures, on golf courses, and on bays. Feeds on grass and other plants. Often forms larger flocks than Canada Geese. May be found in mixed flocks with other goose species at foraging sites.

Look for them at Wireless Road near Astoria, Nestucca Bay National Wildlife Refuge, and Bandon Marsh National Wildlife Refuge. Most only pass through on migration, but a few winter along the coast.

Call varies, but is a high, short yelp.

Similar species: see Canada Goose entry page 51.

Adult with goslings. A large white-cheeked goose with a long, sloping bill. Goslings are yellow, then gray as they grow.

Dusky subspecies. Distinguished by its chocolate brown breast.

CANADA GOOSE

Branta canadensis

A frequent sight in parks and golf courses, this familiar species also includes some subspecies that lead more adventurous lives. Dusky Canada Geese breed on the Copper River Delta in Alaska and winter in the Willamette Valley and at Nestucca Bay National Wildlife Refuge.

Found in pastures, on golf courses, and in freshwater and estuaries. Feeds on grass and other plants. Nest is a pile of vegetation lined with down, built on a platform, small island, or other location that predators cannot reach.

Look for them at Nestucca Bay National Wildlife Refuge, Eckman Lake, and Charleston Boat Basin. Common year-round as both a breeding resident and a winter visitor.

Call is a loud honk that starts with a low grunt and ends higher.

Similar species: see Cackling Goose entry page 49.

Breeding male (left) and female (right). Male is gray with a vertical white bar behind the buffy breast. Pale "taillights." Head is chestnut with a green streak. Female is brown with a dark line through the eye. Both have a green wing patch.

Female Cinnamon Teal. Larger with a longer bill, a paler face, and no "taillights."

GREEN-WINGED TEAL

Anas crecca

This tiny duck often acts like a shorebird, walking across mudflats in groups and pecking at bits of food. Look for their telltale pale yellow "taillights."

Found in bays, estuaries, lakes, and flooded fields. Feeds on plant seeds and invertebrates. Dabbles in shallow water and walks on mudflats. Often found resting along the water's edge.

Look for them at Neskowin Beach Golf Course, Yaquina Bay, and Bandon Marsh National Wildlife Refuge. Uncommon to common September–April.

Males give a chirpy "hee" in courtship that carries well. Females give a quack and a fast chuckle.

Female Cinnamon Teal is rare to uncommon August–May.

LENGTH: 14" / WINGSPAN: 23"

Breeding male.
Green head, white body, cinnamon sides. Large, light blue wing patch visible in flight.

Female.
Brown with an orange bill and a grayish wing patch.

Nonbreeding male.
Males take months to transition from nonbreeding to breeding plumage in the fall. Pale eyes and a dark bill distinguish them from females.

NORTHERN SHOVELER

Spatula clypeata

This odd-looking duck's long, wide bill is equipped with comblike filters that pull small food items from the water. In winter, shovelers form large flocks and feed cooperatively by swimming together in a spiral to stir up food.

Found in marshes, sewage ponds, bays, and lakes. Dabbles for crustaceans and plant matter.

Look for them at Warrenton Waterfront Trail, Salishan Nature Trail, and Millicoma Marsh. Common August–May on the North Coast. Less common on the South Coast.

Males make a squeaky "tsook" call. Females make a long quack.

Similar species: see Mallard entry page 59.

Breeding male.
Gray with a black rump.
Head is puffy, unmarked,
and the bill is dark.
Wing shows chestnut
and white patches.

Female.
Mottled brown with a grayish
face. Thin bill is orange only
on the sides. Legs are yellow.

GADWALL

Mareca strepera

Male Gadwalls are less flashy than most ducks, but a closer look reveals a pattern of fine lines, called vermiculation. The male's quack sounds like a person saying "Hey. Hey. Hey."

 Found in lakes, wetlands, flooded fields, and estuaries. Dabbles for aquatic plants, seeds, and invertebrates. Nests in wetlands, ideally on islands that provide protection from mammalian predators.

Look for them at Astoria Mitigation Bank Wetlands, Eckman Lake, and Bandon Marsh National Wildlife Refuge. Uncommon to common year-round, but less in summer.

Males make a "hee-quack" in courtship that starts with a high whistle. Females make a chuckle and an alarm grunt.

Similar species: see Mallard entry page 59.

Breeding male.
Distinctive green head, yellow bill, and curled black tail feathers. Both sexes have orange legs and a blue wing patch bordered in white.

Female with ducklings.
Warm brown with a tan head, orange-and-black bill.

MALLARD

Anas platyrhynchos

These familiar ducks are easy to find because they happily tolerate human proximity. Take an opportunity to observe them closely and you might notice that the stereotypical "quack" is actually made by the female.

Found in freshwater bodies and estuaries of all sizes, usually near the edges. Also uses temporary wetlands like flooded pastures. Feeds on small invertebrates, plant seeds, and grain. Dabbles in shallow water and also feeds while walking on land. Nest is a broad grass cup lined with down.

Look for them at Necanicum Estuary Natural History Park, Nestucca Bay National Wildlife Refuge, and the Gold Beach harbor. Very common and widespread October–May. Less common in the summer.

Very vocal. Female makes a loud series of nasal quacks. Also gives a chuckle when feeding or being chased by males. Male gives a grating quack and a series of short quacks.

Similar species: see Gadwall entry page 57.

Breeding male.
Pinkish brown with a white and black back end. Top of head is white, and face is green behind the eye. Large white wing patch visible in flight.

Female.
Brown with a mottled gray head and blue bill.

Breeding male Eurasian Wigeon.
Has a reddish brown head with a yellowish forehead, pinkish breast, and gray body.

AMERICAN WIGEON

Mareca americana

Find a large enough flock of these peppy ducks, and it's likely to contain at least one of their Eurasian Wigeon cousins. Where water is too deep for them to reach underwater plants, wigeons follow American Coots and grab the plants that they retrieve while diving.

Found in bays and estuaries. Eats the leaves and stems of plants as well as algae and some invertebrates. Feeds by dabbling but also walks on land to eat grass.

Look for them at Bayocean Peninsula, Mark Hatfield Marine Science Center and Estuary Trail, and Millicoma Marsh. Common October–April. Less common on the South Coast.

Noisy. Males make a nasal "whi-whee-whew" that sounds like a dog's squeaky toy. Females give a low grunt.

Eurasian Wigeon is a rare visitor that shows up in small numbers in flocks of American Wigeon.

Breeding male.
Head is dark reddish brown,
bill is pale blue and black.
White breast and neck stripe.
Rump and tail are black
with long, thin, tail plumes.

Female.
Neck is long and thin.

Female.
Brown with a long, thin, dark bill.

NORTHERN PINTAIL

Anas acuta

Like a flying greyhound, everything about this sleek duck is long, slender, and built for speed. They maintain speeds of around 50 mph during migration and can go much faster in short bursts.

Found in wetlands, flooded fields, and estuaries. Feeds on invertebrates and the seeds of marsh plants by dabbling. Moves around frequently in winter to find flooded habitat.

Look for them at Bayocean Peninsula, Siletz Bay National Wildlife Refuge, and Millicoma Marsh. Uncommon September–April.

During courtship, males make a "whew" call, punctuated with a loud "hee." Females make a rapid chuckle and a hoarse quack.

Similar species: see female Gadwall entry page 57.

LENGTH: 21" (MALE'S TAIL ADDS LENGTH)
WINGSPAN: 34"

Breeding male.
Black overall. Gray flanks make a "fish" shape with a white "tail" forming a spur at the base of the neck. Peaked head and white marks on the bill are distinctive.

Female.
Brownish overall with gray cheeks. Paler brown "fish" pattern on the flanks is faint.

RING-NECKED DUCK

Aythya collaris

This confusingly named duck has a faint neck ring that is almost impossible to see in the field. It often flocks with other species of diving ducks in winter.

 Found in lakes, ponds, and sloughs. Uses smaller bodies of water than scaups. Diet is more vegetarian than that of closely related scaups. Dives frequently for food.

Look for them at Lake Lytle, Eckman Lake, and Westlake County Park. Uncommon to common October–April.

Males make a "whew" call during courtship.

Similar species: see Greater Scaup entry page 67.

Breeding male.
Gray back, white sides, and black rump and chest. Head is rounded with a large bluish bill and can show green iridescence.

Breeding male (left) and female (right).
Female has a white patch behind the bill.

Breeding male Lesser Scaup.
A smaller duck with a smaller head and bill. Head is peaked at the rear of the crown.

GREATER SCAUP

Aythya marila

Bigger in every way than the similar Lesser Scaup, this hardy duck also prefers larger expanses of open water. Scaups present an ID challenge, with many subtle differences helping to distinguish the two species in their frequently mixed flocks.

Found on open water in bays, lakes, and large rivers. More likely to use estuaries than Lesser Scaup. Eats clams, other invertebrates, and plants found by diving. Forms mixed flocks with Lesser Scaup.

Look for them at Fort Clatsop National Memorial on the Netul River Trail, Bayocean Peninsula, and Charleston Boat Basin. Uncommon October–May.

Males make a long "widdoo" call during courtship in spring. Females make a harsh grunt.

Lesser Scaup is uncommon to common October–April.

Breeding male.
Small sea duck with a small bill and round head. Breeding plumage is slate-blue with chestnut patches and bold white stripes.

Female.
Females, juveniles, and non-breeding males are brown with white spots near the bill and behind the eye.

HARLEQUIN DUCK

Histrionicus histrionicus

This small sea duck's unique life history takes it from nesting along rushing mountain streams to spending the winter riding rough seas. In both habitats, it can be found roosting on rocks.

Found in the rocky intertidal area of headlands, islands, and jetties. Eats crabs, barnacles, snails, and fish eggs. Dives for food, using wings and feet for propulsion. Feeds right in the breakers, unlike scoters, which are usually farther out.

Look for them at Haystack Rock near Cannon Beach, Yaquina Head Outstanding Natural Area, and Cape Arago State Park. Rare to uncommon year-round. Non-breeders summer at the coast in low numbers.

Not usually heard on wintering grounds, but flocks communicate with squeaky "yaps."

Similar species: see female Surf Scoter entry page 71 and female Bufflehead entry page 75.

LENGTH: 16.5" / WINGSPAN: 26"

Male.
Colorful, bulbous bill. Black body with white patches on nape, forehead, and bill.

Female.
Dark brown with white dot on the cheek and vertical white splotch behind the bill.

SURF SCOTER

Melanitta perspicillata

Our most common scoter can be spotted just behind the breakers, where it gathers in large winter flocks. Scan these flocks for the rarer White-winged and Black Scoters.

Found in the nearshore ocean and in bays and estuaries. Dives to feed on mussels, clams, snails, and crabs. Gathers by the hundreds to eat herring eggs during the fish's early spring spawning.

Look for them at Cape Meares State Park, Strawberry Hill Wayside, and Port Orford Heads State Park. Common October–April. Uncommon in summer.

Not usually heard on wintering grounds.

Similar species: see female White-winged Scoter entry page 73.

Male.
Bill is long and tapered with an orange tip. Dash of white behind the eye.

Female.
Dark brown with two round white dots on the face.

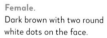

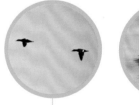

Male (left) and female (right).
Distinctive white wing patches in all plumages.

Male Black Scoter.
Solid black with a yellow-orange knob on the bill.

Female Black Scoter.
Brown with pale cheeks.

WHITE-WINGED SCOTER

Melanitta deglandi

Our largest scoter is also the hardiest, foraging farther from shore, diving deeper, and choosing larger prey. The similar Black Scoter sticks to shallower water.

Found in the ocean and in the lower reaches of estuaries. Eats mollusks, including mussels, that it pulls off rocks while diving. Flocks can be seen flying over the ocean in spring and fall.

Look for them at Ecola State Park, Umpqua River South Jetty, and Chetco Point Park. Uncommon to common September–April.

Not usually heard on wintering grounds.

Black Scoter is rare to uncommon September–April.

LENGTH: 21" / WINGSPAN: 34"

Breeding male.
Small duck with a white body, black back, distinctive white head patch, and iridescent black face. Very visible even at a distance.

Female.
Females and young males are gray below with darker backs and heads. Distinctive oval white spot behind the eye.

BUFFLEHEAD

Bucephala albeola

This ubiquitous duck gets its name from the resemblance of its oversized head to that of a buffalo. They are abundant winter residents on the coast and move up to mountain lakes to breed.

Found on lakes, ponds, bays, estuaries, and slow-moving rivers. Eats a mix of plants and small aquatic animals found by diving. Often in small numbers on small bodies of water, and in larger numbers on bays.

Look for them at Netarts Bay, Alsea Bay Boat Docks, and Bandon Marsh National Wildlife Refuge. Very common November–April.

Not vocal on wintering grounds.

Similar species: see Harlequin Duck entry page 69.

LENGTH: 13.5" / WINGSPAN: 21"

Breeding male.
Head is dark, iridescent green with a round, white spot behind a sloped bill.

Female.
Gray with a brown head. Bill is mostly black with a little yellow.

Breeding male Barrow's Goldeneye.
White crescent on face and more extensive black on back than Common.

Female Barrow's Goldeneye.
Bill is stubbier with more yellow than Common.

COMMON GOLDENEYE

Bucephala clangula

Bright white plumage and comical courtship displays make this duck stand out from the crowd. Common Goldeneyes are more common than Barrow's at the coast in winter, but Barrow's are the only goldeneyes that breed in Oregon.

Found in bays and estuaries. Dives to prey on a variety of marine animals. Begins head-cocking courtship displays while still on wintering grounds.

Look for them at Garibaldi Marina, Salishan Nature Trail, and Millicoma Marsh. Uncommon November–April.

Male gives a nighthawk-like "pi-peent" call as part of courtship display. Females make a harsh grunt.

Barrow's Goldeneye is rare November–April.

LENGTH: 18.5" / WINGSPAN: 26"

Breeding male.
White body with a dark back and dark green head. Long, reddish orange bill.

Female or nonbreeding male.
Gray with a dark reddish brown head and a white chin patch. Short crest on the back of the head.

COMMON MERGANSER

Mergus merganser

This duck's white plumage is visible from a great distance and is sometimes tinged with a salmon color. They gather in large flocks where fish are abundant.

Found mostly in freshwater, but sometimes ventures into estuaries. Eats fish, shrimp, clams, and crabs found by snorkeling with its face in the water. Breeds along rivers. Prefers hollow trees for nesting, but also nests on the ground in the shelter of rocks or brush.

Look for them at Cape Meares Lake, East Devil's Lake State Recreation Area, and the Gold Beach marina. Uncommon to common October–April; rare otherwise.

Males give a low "g'daa" call during courtship.

Similar species: see Red-breasted Merganser entry page 81.

LENGTH: 25" / WINGSPAN: 34"

Breeding male.
Plumage is a patchwork of brown, black, white, and gray. Dark green head, shaggy crest, thin, reddish orange bill.

Female.
Females and nonbreeding males are gray and white with orangish brown heads and crests.

RED-BREASTED MERGANSER

Mergus serrator

These spiky seagoing ducks work cooperatively to herd and catch fish. They are usually seen singly or in small flocks.

 Found primarily in saltwater, but often chooses the shelter of bays and river mouths over the open ocean. Eats fish, crustaceans, worms, and other aquatic creatures found by snorkeling and diving.

Look for them at Bayocean Peninsula, Siuslaw River South Jetty, and Coquille River South Jetty. Uncommon October–May.

Males give a "whiddew" call during courtship.

Similar species: see Common Merganser entry page 79.

Adult.
Pale bill has a dark band. Bill comes to a dark point between the red eyes.

Adult.
Dark plumage and yellow legs with lobed toes.

AMERICAN COOT

Fulica americana

It's easy to imagine coots as clowns with their big feet, awkward movements, and undignified noises. They bob their heads forward when swimming or walking, making them easily identifiable from a distance.

Found in freshwater wetlands, bays, and estuaries. Eats aquatic plants and algae obtained on land or by diving. Wigeons and Gadwalls follow them to take advantage of the food they bring up from below.

Look for them at Young's Bay, Bayocean Peninsula, and Millicoma Marsh. Common September–April; rare in the breeding season.

Often vocal while foraging. Emits a variety of squawking honks, snorts, and barks, sometimes in a series.

Dark plumage, pale bill, and lobed feet distinguish it from ducks.

LENGTH: 15.5" / WINGSPAN: 24"

Breeding adult.
Slim loon with a thin bill held up at an angle. Body is dark, head and neck are gray with a red throat patch.

Nonbreeding adult.
Distinctive white face and neck with a black crown and nape. Back has white speckles.

RED-THROATED LOON

Gavia stellata

This loon's scientific name refers poetically to the constellation of starlike white speckles on its back. A distinguishing feature in flight is that its neck hangs lower than other loon species.

Found in the ocean and in bays. Often forages near shore where it can be easily seen. Eats a variety of fish species caught by diving.

Look for them at Seaside Cove, Barview Jetty, and Cape Arago State Park. Uncommon to common in winter; rare in summer.

Mostly quiet away from breeding grounds but may give a "quack."

Similar species: see Pacific Loon entry page 87.

Breeding adult. Distinctive pale gray nape.

Nonbreeding adult. Nonbreeding and juvenile plumages have a gray head, rounded nape, white chin, and white throat. Nonbreeding adults show a dark chinstrap.

PACIFIC LOON

Gavia pacifica

During migration, these loons move along the Oregon Coast in huge numbers, with over 40,000 recorded on one spring day from a single viewpoint. Look for them in long, loose flocks flying low over the ocean.

Found in the ocean and in bays and lower estuaries. Eats small fish found by diving frequently.

Look for them at Fort Stevens State Park—South Jetty, Boiler Bay State Wayside, and Port Orford. Common in spring and fall migration.

Mostly quiet away from breeding grounds but may give a "whoop" or a bark.

Similar species: see Common Loon entry page 89.

Breeding adult.
Large, chunky loon with a blocky head and heavy bill. Breeding plumage is sharply patterned in black and white, including a white collar and checkering on the back.

Nonbreeding adult.
Nonbreeding and juvenile plumages are gray with white around the eye, a white chin, and a partial collar.

COMMON LOON

Gavia immer

We rarely hear this loon's iconic song in Oregon, but we can enjoy watching them feast on fish and crabs in coastal bays and harbors. Eating fish near shore makes Common Loons vulnerable to ingesting lead fishing weights and becoming tangled in abandoned fishing line.

Found in the ocean and in bays and estuaries. In winter, it is sometimes found in rivers and lakes. More likely to be found in freshwater than other loons. Eats fish, crabs, mollusks, and other marine life. Snorkels with face in the water, and dives to find food.

Look for them at Nehalem Bay State Park, Yaquina Bay South Jetty, and Chetco Point Park. Common except in June–August when only nonbreeding birds remain.

Mostly quiet away from breeding grounds but may give a "whoop."

Similar species: see Pacific Loon entry page 87.

LENGTH: 32" / WINGSPAN: 46"

Dark eye, thick pale bill with a black stripe, black chin.

Plumage is warm brown and darker above. Rump is pale and fluffy in both plumages.

PIED-BILLED GREBE

Podilymbus podiceps

This inconspicuous freshwater grebe stays in more sheltered habitats than its seafaring cousins. When threatened, it adjusts its feathers to change its buoyancy and sinks under the water to escape.

Found mostly in freshwater wetlands and slow-moving water. Eats fish, crustaceans, and insects obtained by diving. Nest is a floating mat of vegetation.

Look for them at Cannon Beach Settling Ponds, East Devil's Lake State Recreation Area, and Eckman Lake. Uncommon August–April; rare in the breeding season.

Song is a long series of loud whoops that sound like something you'd hear in a tropical rainforest. Pairs also perform chatter duets on their territory. Juveniles beg loudly with a series of "pseeps."

Similar species: see Horned Grebe entry page 93.

LENGTH: 13" / WINGSPAN: 16"

Breeding adult.
Small grebe with a flat head.
Black with a reddish neck and
thick yellow stripe behind the eye.

Nonbreeding adult.
Usually seen in nonbreeding plumage with a white neck and cheek and
a crisp black cap. Bill has a whitish tip.

Nonbreeding adult Eared Grebe.
Slimmer overall with a slightly
upturned bill. The head peaks
above the eye. Face is smudged.

HORNED GREBE

Podiceps auritus

This fluffy little grebe is less wary than most and can be easily viewed in bays and rivers. Seen close to shore, sometimes among other grebes.

Winters in bays and estuaries and in the nearshore ocean. Winter diet is fish and shrimp caught while diving. Found singly or in small, loose flocks.

Look for them at Netarts Bay, Salmon Harbor Marina, and Port of Brookings Harbor. Uncommon to common September–April.

May make a screechy wail in late winter.

Eared Grebe is rare to uncommon September–April.

Breeding adult. Breeding plumage is dark with a red neck, white face, and black cap. Thick neck and large, yellow bill.

Nonbreeding adult. Plumage is shades of brown and gray with a dark cap and paler chin and neck.

RED-NECKED GREBE

Podiceps grisegena

These sturdy grebes visit Oregon in the winter when their northern breeding lakes are frozen over. They can be seen diving repeatedly, propelling themselves underwater with their feet and grabbing prey with their pointed bills.

Winters in sheltered waters in the ocean and in bays. Dives to catch fish. Usually solitary in winter, except where food is abundant.

Look for them at Barview Jetty, Yaquina Bay South Jetty, and Charleston Boat Basin. Uncommon to common August–May.

Mostly silent in winter.

Similar species: see Western Grebe entry page 97 and Horned Grebe entry page 93.

LENGTH: 18" / WINGSPAN: 24"

Nonbreeding adult.
Long, thin neck and a red eye. Long bill is greenish yellow. Face has more black on it in breeding plumage.

Nonbreeding adult Clark's Grebe.
Black cap does not envelop the eye. Bill is orangish yellow.

WESTERN GREBE

Aechmophorus occidentalis

They don't perform their jaw-dropping water dancing display at the Oregon Coast, but rafts of them floating in the ocean are still an impressive sight. You will almost always see them on the water because they migrate at night and do not walk on land.

Winters in bays and in the nearshore ocean. Primarily feeds on fish obtained by diving. Gathers in large numbers in the winter.

Look for them at Seaside Cove, Yaquina Head Outstanding Natural Area, and Cape Blanco State Park. Common October–April; rare otherwise.

Song, a "krik-kreek," is sometimes heard in winter.

Clark's Grebe is rare but sometimes present in large flocks of Westerns.

LENGTH: 25" / WINGSPAN: 24"

Breeding adult.
Blue throat pouch and white, whisker-like plumes on the head and shoulders.

Breeding adult.
Performing a courtship display.

Nonbreeding adult.
Face is dark with a distinctive buffy cheek patch.

BRANDT'S CORMORANT

Urile penicillatus

This drab bird gets a colorful makeover each breeding season before performing its eye-catching courtship displays. During their performances they flap their wings, arch their necks, and flutter their bright blue throat patches.

Found in the ocean, and occasionally in bays and estuaries. Seen flying low over the ocean in single-file lines. Eats a variety of fish caught by swimming underwater with webbed feet. Nests on offshore rocks and cliffs, occasionally on pilings. Nest is made from seaweed and vegetation collected near the nest site.

Look for them at Haystack Rock near Cannon Beach, Yaquina Head Outstanding Natural Area, and Harris Beach State Park. Common May–September; uncommon otherwise.

Grunts while on its nesting colony.

Similar species: see Pelagic Cormorant entry page 101 and Double-crested Cormorant entry page 103.

LENGTH: 34" / WINGSPAN: 48"

Breeding adult.
Two shaggy spikes on the head, red skin around the eye, and fine white plumes on the neck.

Breeding adult.
In flight, shows a large white patch on each flank.

Nonbreeding adult.
Glossy black plumage shines green and purple. Bill is thin and dark.

PELAGIC CORMORANT

Urile pelagicus

Despite its name, this small cormorant is not found far out to sea but near the coast and in bays and estuaries. Its sleek silhouette and thin, snakelike neck are distinctive as it dives in the surf.

Found near shore and in bays and estuaries. Eats fish and crustaceans found while swimming underwater. Nests in small colonies on cliffs, ledges, and bridges. Nest is made from seaweed and plants and cemented to the nest site with guano. Breeding birds perform courtship displays by waving their wings and head.

Look for them at Cape Meares State Park, Boiler Bay State Scenic Viewpoint, and Cape Arago State Park. Common to very common year-round.

Honks and moans on the nest.

Similar species: see Brandt's Cormorant entry page 99 and Double-crested Cormorant entry page 103.

LENGTH: 28" / WINGSPAN: 39"

Breeding adult.
Plumes on the sides of the head.

Nonbreeding adult.
Blackish brown with orange skin on face and throat. Head is blocky, and neck is kinked in flight.

Juvenile.
Brown with a paler breast.

DOUBLE-CRESTED CORMORANT

Nannopterum auritum

Easy to take for granted, this ubiquitous waterbird rewards closer examination with jewellike blue eyes complemented by an orange face. This fish eater is sometimes scapegoated for fish declines that have more complex causes.

Nests on offshore rocks, pilings, and sandy islands, but usually commutes to freshwater to forage. Hunts by swimming underwater, eating whatever fish are available. Breeds in colonies and makes nests from plant material. Roosts on pilings, on rocks, and in trees.

Look for them at Fort Stevens State Park, Mark Hatfield Marine Science Center and Estuary Trail, and Port of Brookings Harbor. Common to very common year-round.

Gives croaks and grunts while in the nesting colony.

Similar species: see Pelagic Cormorant entry page 101 and Brandt's Cormorant entry page 99.

Nonbreeding adult.
Very large bird with a
white head and neck,
a long, pouched bill,
and webbed feet.

Breeding adult.
Yellow head, black neck, and red pouch.
This plumage is rarely seen in Oregon.

Juvenile.
Brown with a white belly.

**Nonbreeding adult
American White Pelican.**
Larger than Brown Pelican,
with white plumage and black
wing feathers. Bill and pouch
are yellow, feet are orange.

BROWN PELICAN

Pelecanus occidentalis

These ancient-looking birds visit Oregon for a yearly fishing trip after breeding in California. Their population has now recovered from the catastrophic effects of the pesticide DDT on fish-eating birds.

Found in the nearshore ocean area and in bays and estuaries. Roosts on offshore rocks and jetties. Eats small fish like anchovies. Catches fish by diving from the air and opening its pouch as it plunges into the water bill-first. Flies in lines, often low over the ocean to ride the air currents off the waves.

Look for them at Haystack Rock near Pacific City, Fort Stevens State Park: South Jetty, and Cape Arago State Park. Very common May–October; rare otherwise.

Usually silent away from breeding grounds.

American White Pelican is occasionally found on the North Coast, especially in the Columbia River Estuary.

Adult.
Large, chunky shorebird with brownish black plumage. Red-orange bill and orange skin around yellow eyes. Legs are pale pink.

Juvenile.
Darker bill with gray at the tip.

BLACK OYSTERCATCHER

Haematopus bachmani

An oystercatcher blends in with the dark basalt rocks that it forages and nests on, but loud calls and a brightly colored bill give its presence away. That carrotlike bill is its most prominent feature and most important tool for making a living in the rocky intertidal zone.

Found on rocky habitats including outcroppings, islands, and jetties. Rarely seen on sandy beaches. Eats intertidal invertebrates including bivalves, limpets, crabs, barnacles, and worms (but not oysters) using its flattened, sharp bill. Nests are located on rocks near the intertidal area and are made of rock and shell pieces.

Look for them at Haystack Rock near Cannon Beach, Boiler Bay State Scenic Viewpoint, and Coquille River jetties. Common year-round. Breeds in higher numbers on the South Coast.

Calls are "peeps" and "weews" that are sometimes strung together into a series.

Dark plumage is unique among shorebirds, but they could be mistaken for crows in distant flight.

LENGTH: 17.5" / WINGSPAN: 32"

Breeding male.
Solid black belly, chest, and face with a white undertail. Black "armpits" unique among similar plovers. Female is grayish with a splotchy black belly.

Nonbreeding adult.
White below, mottled gray above with a pale eyebrow.

Juvenile.
Speckled back and streaked breast.

BLACK-BELLIED PLOVER

Pluvialis squatarola

The largest plover in North America spends the winter along the coast, where its gray plumage matches the weather. Its large size and active feeding behavior make it easy to spot.

Prefers muddy habitats like tidal mudflats and bare fields but can also be found on sandy beaches. Eats invertebrates including bivalves and marine worms.

Look for them at Del Rey Beach, Salishan Nature Trail, and Mark Hatfield Marine Science Center and Estuary Trail. Rare to uncommon year-round, except during summer. Most common April–May in migration.

Distinctive "pyoowee" call helps to distinguish it from similar plovers. Also gives "peer" and "pip" calls.

Black-bellied is the largest, heaviest billed, and by far the most common of a trio of similar plovers that includes Pacific Golden-Plover and American Golden-Plover, both rare.

Breeding adult.
Black on the forehead,
ear patch, and collar.

Nonbreeding adult.
Incomplete collar, gray
legs, small black bill.

Pair at a nest.

WESTERN SNOWY PLOVER

Charadrius nivosus nivosus

This threatened subspecies of Snowy Plover is a conservation success story. Oregon's only shorebird that nests on sandy beaches, it is now easier to find than it has been in decades.

Requires broad, sandy beaches with gently sloping dunes. Eats small invertebrates found among tidal debris. Lays eggs in a sandy depression, depending on shells, wood, and plants to offer camouflage for exposed eggs and chicks. Runs quickly on short legs, scooting along as if on wheels.

Look for them at Nehalem Bay State Park, Sitka Sedge State Natural Area, and around the Siltcoos River mouth. Rare to uncommon year-round.

Whistles a "ter-weet" call during courtship and may let out a "burrt" or "cheep" call if disturbed.

Similar species: see Semipalmated Plover entry page 113 and Sanderling entry page 127.

Breeding adult.
Bill is orange
with black tip.

Nonbreeding adult.
Single breastband
and distinctive yellow
legs. A dark mask cov-
ers the eyes leaving a
white spot over the bill.

SEMIPALMATED PLOVER

Charadrius semipalmatus

Look for these busy little plovers mixed in with flocks of migrating sandpipers. Their round shape and short bill make them easy to distinguish.

Forages on mudflats and sandy beaches. Runs around open areas, where it pecks and probes for invertebrates, including worms.

Look for them at Fort Stevens State Park: Parking Area D, Brian Booth State Park, and Bandon Marsh National Wildlife Refuge. Common April–May and July–September when they migrate through Oregon.

Call is a "peweep" or "peep."

Similar species: see Snowy Plover entry page 111 and Killdeer entry page 115.

LENGTH: 7.25" / WINGSPAN: 19"

Adult.
Two black bands across the chest, white collar, and pink legs.

Adult.
In flight, a rufous rump and black tail band are visible.

KILLDEER

Charadrius vociferus

Nervous and noisy, they give their namesake song frequently as they watch for threats. Their well-known broken-wing display lures predators away from their nest.

Found in areas with sparse or low vegetation, often near water, but also favors human-made areas like parking lots, fields, roadsides, golf courses, and airports. Nests on bare or rocky ground in a scrape it may line with pebbles. Diet includes a variety of invertebrates.

Look for them along bays, rivers and in grassy fields. Common year-round. More are found at the coast when winter weather is cold inland.

Named for its repeated "kill-DEER" song. Give several other calls and alarms including "deet," "dit," and a long twitter.

Similar species: see Semipalmated Plover entry page 113.

Adult.
Head is striped, including a pale stripe on the crown. Legs are long and gray. Bill is long and curves down.

Adult Long-billed Curlew.
Even longer bill and cinnamon underwings. Lacks a crown stripe.

WHIMBREL

Numenius phaeopus

This distinctive shorebird patrols beaches in search of the seasonal bounty of mole crabs, a vital fuel for migration. Usually seen in flocks during migration and may mix with Marbled Godwits.

Found on sandy ocean beaches, estuary mudflats, and in coastal pastures. Forages at the edge of the ocean but also higher on the beach where debris collects. Walks methodically when foraging, using its long bill to peck at surface arthropods and probe for buried crabs, worms, and mollusks.

Look for them at Del Rey Beach, South Beach State Park, and Bandon State Natural Area. Present March–September and common April–May.

A series of "peep," "pip," or "keek" calls is given in alarm and flight.

Long-billed Curlew is rare in spring and fall.

Breeding adult.
Breast and belly marbled
with dark bars. Long
bill with orange base
curves slightly upward.
Underwings buffy orange.

Juvenile or nonbreeding adult.
Plumage is buffy with an
unmarked breast and belly.
Bill has a pink base.

MARBLED GODWIT

Limosa fedoa

Few worms are out of reach for this enthusiastic long-billed mud prober. Godwits linger on the Oregon Coast in fall and can still be found in October.

Found feeding on sandy beaches and mudflats and roosting in fields and on jetties. Feeds by probing into mud or sand with its long bill, all the way up to its face. Also wades in water, submerging its head to feed. Eats worms, clams, and crabs. Usually found as singles or in small flocks.

Look for them at Fort Stevens State Park: Parking Area D, Mark Hatfield Marine Science Center and Estuary Trail, and Bandon Marsh National Wildlife Refuge. Rare April–May; uncommon July–October.

"Reek" and "reek-reek" calls given in alarm and in flight.

Other species of godwits are very rare in Oregon and lack the buffy coloration and orangish underwings of Marbled Godwits.

Nonbreeding adult.
Bold black-and-white
pattern on back and
wings in flight. Legs
are dark. Bill is pointed.
Breeding plumage has
more white on the face.

**Nonbreeding adult
Ruddy Turnstone.**
Brightly patterned rufous,
black, and white breed-
ing plumage gives way to
grayish brown nonbreed-
ing plumage with dark
markings on the breast.

BLACK TURNSTONE

Arenaria melanocephala

These round rockpipers scurry and jump to stay just beyond the ocean's reach. They are busy, noisy foragers that are often found in mixed flocks with Surfbirds.

Found on rock outcroppings and cobbled beaches. Picks at invertebrates on intertidal rocks, turning aside seaweed and debris (but not stones) in its search. Blends in with dark gray basalt rock when roosting at high tide.

Look for them at Yachats State Park, Seaside Cove, and jetties, including the Rogue River South Jetty. Very common in rocky intertidal areas late July–April.

Chitter loudly to each other while foraging and in flight. Give "keer" and "reek" calls in alarm.

Ruddy Turnstone is a rare visitor in spring and fall. Similar species: see also Surfbird entry page 123.

Breeding adult.
Rufous shoulders and black spots on the breast and belly.

Nonbreeding adult.
Gray above and white below with some dark speckles. Bill is yellow and black and relatively stubby. Legs are yellow.

Nonbreeding adult Rock Sandpiper.
Long, drooping bill with a yellow base.

SURFBIRD

Calidris virgata

Earns its name dodging breaking waves to forage at the ocean's rocky edge. Less vocal and frenetic than Black Turnstone, so it may not stand out as easily from the rocks.

 Forages in rocky intertidal areas like jetties and tidepools, often associated with Black Turnstones. Plucks barnacles, mussels, and snails off rocks with its blunt, thick bill.

 Look for them at Barview Jetty, Seal Rock State Park, and Coquille River South Jetty. Common in rocky intertidal habitats late July–April.

🎵 Not very vocal in winter but gives a "cheep" call.

🍃 Rock Sandpiper (rare) associates with Surfbirds in winter. Also similar species: see Black Turnstone entry page 121.

Identification of common sandpipers

Sandpipers, especially the small ones known as "peeps," are known for presenting some identification puzzles. Start by looking at bill shape and leg color to narrow down the choices.

SPECIES	LEG COLOR	RELATIVE SIZE	BILL	PLUMAGE	SOUNDS	SEASONAL ABUNDANCE
LEAST SANDPIPER	yellow or yellow-green	small	short with a slight droop and a thin tip	brown hood extending over chest	high "breet"	common in spring and fall; uncommon in winter
WESTERN SANDPIPER	black	small	long and drooping	white face and chest; rusty shoulder stripe on juveniles	high "cheep"	common in spring and fall; rare in winter
SANDERLING	black	medium	short and straight	white and pale gray much of the year	clear "wink"	common late July–April; rare otherwise
DUNLIN	black	medium	very long and drooping	black belly in summer	scratchy screech and an excited twitter	somewhat common late September–May; rare otherwise

Breeding male.
Rufous head, neck
and back. Female
has less rufous.

Nonbreeding adult.
Pale gray above and white below,
with black shoulders. Black legs
and a short, straight bill.

Juvenile.
White below and speckled
black and white on the back.

SANDERLING

Calidris alba

In perpetual motion, they scurry up and down the beach with the waves. A very close look reveals that Sanderlings lack the hind toe typical of sandpipers.

Found on sandy ocean beaches, especially where there are long open stretches of beach. Roosts on dry sand at high tide. Forages for amphipods and small clams in the wet sand right at the edge of the waves. In peak migration, found in flocks of hundreds or even thousands of birds.

Look for them at Sunset Beach Recreation Area, Sitka Sedge State Natural Area, and Bullards Beach State Park. Uncommon to common late July–April.

Call is a clear "wink." Gives a "twitter" call when interacting.

See Western Sandpiper entry page 133.

Breeding adult. Long, drooping bill and dark legs. Black belly and rufous back make their breeding plumage distinctive.

Nonbreeding adult. Plumage is gray-brown above and on the breast.

DUNLIN

Calidris alpina

Synchronized flocks of Dunlin are a mesmerizing sight, turning from gray to white as they swirl over a mudflat. They fly in these cohesive flocks to avoid predation from Merlins and Peregrine Falcons.

Gathers to feed in large flocks on mudflats. Roosts on beaches, rocks, and in fields at high tide. Probes for arthropods, worms, and clams.

Look for them at Fort Stevens State Park: Parking Area D, Bayocean Peninsula, and Bandon Marsh National Wildlife Refuge. Uncommon to common late September–May.

A long, scratchy "grate" call is given in flight and alarm.

Similar species: see Western Sandpiper entry page 133.

Breeding adult.
Brown on the back, wings, and breast gives it a distinctive hooded look. Legs yellow or greenish yellow. Bill relatively short and droops slightly to a fine point.

Nonbreeding adult.
Grayish brown and darker than other peeps.

Juvenile.
Rufous back.

LEAST SANDPIPER

Calidris minutilla

Our smallest sandpiper is easily found in even the smallest ponds and puddles, making it a good starter shorebird. Associates with Semipalmated Plovers and other small sandpipers in mixed flocks.

Found in freshwater wetlands, puddles, estuaries, and less often on sandy beaches. Feeds in muddy areas, often near the edge of the water where there is low vegetation. Rarely wades. Eats a wide variety of prey including amphipods, snails, and flies. Crouches to feed because of its short bill.

Look for them at Sitka Sedge Natural Area, Salishan Nature Trail, and Coquille River South Jetty. Common during spring and fall migration; uncommon in winter.

High "breet" call given in flight.

Similar species: see Western Sandpiper entry page 133.

Breeding adult.
Rufous on the shoulders,
cap, and cheeks as well
as spotting on the chest.

Nonbreeding adult.
Gray above and white below.
Long, drooping bill and black legs.

Juvenile.
Grayish plumage, dis-
tinctive rufous shoulders
and a pale face and
chest. Juveniles arrive
beginning in July.

**Breeding adult Semi-
palmated Sandpiper.**
Shorter, blunter bill
and darker cap than
Western Sandpiper.

**Juvenile Baird's
Sandpiper.**
Buffy breast. Back and
wings appear "scaly." Wingtips extend beyond the tail.

WESTERN SANDPIPER

Calidris mauri

As one of Oregon's most common sandpipers, it plays a large part in the spectacle of shorebird migration. Westerns can be a challenge to separate from several other small sandpipers. See table on page 125 for a summary of key field marks.

Large flocks are found on mudflats and beaches during migration, where they probe for worms, mollusks, and crustaceans. May be seen in mixed flocks with other shorebirds.

Look for them at Bayocean Peninsula, Umpqua River South Jetty, and Bandon Marsh National Wildlife Refuge. Common April–May and July–September. Rare in winter.

Call is a high "cheep" or "breet," usually given while in flight.

Semipalmated Sandpiper is rare during spring and fall migration. Baird's Sandpiper is rare to uncommon August–September.

LENGTH: 6.5" / WINGSPAN: 14"

Breeding adult. Rusty with black spots along the sides of the breast. Back feathers have buffy bars and edges.

Nonbreeding adult. Grayish with a white belly and a pale eyebrow. Slimmer body overall than Long-billed.

Breeding adult Long-billed Dowitcher. Rusty with dark streaks along the sides of the breast. Back feathers are dark with rusty spots and white edges.

Nonbreeding adult Long-billed Dowitcher. Grayish with a white belly and a pale eyebrow. Rounder breast and more humped back than Short-billed.

SHORT-BILLED DOWITCHER

Limnodromus griseus

With their bills buried deep in the mud, you'll have to use other clues to tell the Short-billed Dowitcher from its Long-billed doppelgänger. Both species have greenish yellow legs and a large white patch on the lower back in flight.

Short-billeds forage on mudflats and in shallow water and roost on jetties, while Long-billeds prefer ponds and flooded pastures. Both wade and feed by rapidly probing in mud (think sewing machine needle) and eat a variety of invertebrates.

Look for them at Fort Stevens State Park, Mark Hatfield Marine Science Center and Estuary Trail, and Bandon Marsh National Wildlife Refuge. Both are uncommon in migration April–May and July–September. Long-billed is also present in winter.

Short-billed gives a series of "pew" calls and a whistled "pee." Long-billed gives a high "peep" call that turns into a twitter when excited.

Long-billed Dowitcher can be differentiated based on plumage and sounds.

LENGTH: 11" / WINGSPAN: 19"

Breeding female. Red neck, white throat, needlelike bill. Females are larger and are more boldly colored in breeding plumage than males.

Nonbreeding adult. Streaked gray above, white below, with a black smudge behind the eye.

Nonbreeding adult Red Phalarope. Paler gray with a thicker bill.

RED-NECKED PHALAROPE

Phalaropus lobatus

Phalaropes are even more at home in the water than they are on land. They spin and paddle their feet while swimming to stir up food.

Forages in sewage ponds and bays. Also found along ocean beaches and at sea. Eats a wide variety of foods depending on foraging habitat, picking small food items from the water's surface. Usually occurs in small flocks.

Look for them at Nehalem Sewage Ponds (restricted access), Salishan Nature Trail, and the Coos Bay North Spit: Weyco Settling Pond. Rare to uncommon April–May and July–October.

Call is a sharp "pip."

Red Phalarope is rarely seen from shore October–December and gets blown ashore during storms.

Breeding adult.
Black spots on a white
breast. Dark line through
the eye and a white eyering.
Bill is orange with a dark tip.

Nonbreeding adult.
Brown above and white
below. Bill is yellowish.

SPOTTED SANDPIPER

Actitis macularius

A unique sandpiper that breeds near the coast and frequents rivers and other freshwater habitats. In its trademark behavior, the back half of the bird teeters up and down constantly while it walks.

Found in a variety of fresh and saltwater habitats. Walks quickly along the edge of the water and picks at aquatic and terrestrial prey. Nests near water and conceals the nest in vegetation. Male may do a Killdeer-like feigned injury display if a threat is detected near the nest. In flight, wingbeats are shallow and fluttery.

Look for them at Cannon Beach Settling Ponds, Brian Booth State Park, and Chetco Point Park. Uncommon to common year-round.

Often vocal in flight. Song is a rapid series of "weep" notes. Call is "pee-pwee-pwee" or a series of "pips."

Similar species: see Least Sandpiper entry page 131 and Solitary Sandpiper photo page 142

Breeding adult.
Underparts narrowly barred in white and gray.

Nonbreeding adult.
Long bill and yellow legs. Gray overall with only a little white on chin and underparts.

WANDERING TATTLER

Tringa incana

An aptly named rockpiper that visits Oregon on its travels between Alaska and the South Pacific. Its gray plumage blends well with basalt rocks, but its presence is betrayed by an active feeding style and loud calls.

Found on rocky shores, and sometimes on rocks in estuaries. Eats a variety of invertebrate prey picked from the rocks at low tide. Teeters its back end up and down while walking, similar to Spotted Sandpiper.

Look for them at Barview Jetty, Yachats State Park, and Coquille River jetties. Uncommon late April–May and July–September. Rare in winter.

Call, given in flight and alarm, is "pee-pee-pee."

Similar species: see Surfbird entry page 123.

Breeding adult.
Darker with barring on the sides.

Nonbreeding adult.
Long, yellow legs. Bill is longer than the head and looks slightly upturned. Plumage streaked in gray with white underparts.

Breeding adult Lesser Yellowlegs.
Smaller with a straight, needlelike bill approximately the length of the head.

Breeding adult Solitary Sandpiper.
Greenish legs. Dark back has small white spots.

GREATER YELLOWLEGS

Tringa melanoleuca

These brash birds often announce their presence by chasing each other around and calling loudly. They are found in small groups that may also include Lesser Yellowlegs.

Forage in open areas with shallow water including ponds, freshwater wetlands, estuaries, and flooded fields. They are active foragers that wade in water and run after prey such as small fish, crustaceans, and snails.

Look for them at Sitka Sedge State Natural Area, Eckman Lake, and Bandon Marsh National Wildlife Refuge. Uncommon to common July–May. Winter in small numbers at the coast.

Calls frequently in flight, most commonly a "klee" series. May also give a slurred "kleer" series in alarm. Lesser Yellowlegs' alarm call is a "pew."

Lesser Yellowlegs is rare to uncommon in spring and fall. Solitary Sandpiper is rare.

LENGTH: 14" / WINGSPAN: 28"

Adult.
Blue-gray overall with a long, pointed bill. Black plumes decorate the head.

Adult.
Flies with long neck tucked in and long legs straight out behind.

GREAT BLUE HERON

Ardea herodias

This bird's iconic silhouette is a familiar sight up and down the Oregon Coast. North America's largest heron, the Great Blue can swallow surprisingly hefty prey.

Hunts in a variety of fresh and saltwater habitats and in open fields. Feeds at low tide, preferring to hunt in water that is about a foot deep. Eats fish, frogs, small mammals, and occasionally birds. Nests colonially in rookeries, building stick nests in trees. Also roosts in trees.

Look for them in bays, rivers, and wetlands. Very common year-round.

Most commonly heard call is an alarm croak.

There are no other large, grayish herons in western Oregon.

Adult.
Long black legs and a long, pointed, yellow bill. Head is smooth with no plumes.

Adult.
Flies with long neck tucked in and long legs straight out behind.

GREAT EGRET

Ardea alba

Standing out in pure white plumage, they gather by the dozens in coastal fields and estuaries each winter. Egrets have recovered well from the population crash caused by hunting for the plume trade over a century ago.

Hunts in marshes, streams, ponds, and fields. Diet is flexible, including fish, amphibians, small mammals, insects, and more. Makes stick nests in trees and may share rookeries with Great Blue Herons.

Look for them in Tillamook Bay and the farm fields to the east, Netarts Bay, and Yaquina Bay. Common with a dip in abundance April–July.

Croaks and grunts are given in alarm.

The only egret regularly found at the coast.

Adult.
Long, pointed wings that join at the midpoint of the body. Wing linings are silvery. Bill is thin and hooked.

A large flock of shearwaters passes by close to shore.

SOOTY SHEARWATER

Ardenna grisea

Shearwaters are long-distance travelers that pass by the coast on their never-ending journey around the Pacific Ocean in search of a good meal. At peak times in fall, flocks of thousands continuously pass by the Oregon Coast.

Found flying over the ocean, sometimes close to shore. Eats fish, squid, and crustaceans plucked off the surface or grabbed while diving underwater. Flight style is distinctive even at a distance: a few flaps followed by a stiff-winged glide very low over the waves.

Look for them just offshore from Fort Stevens State Park: South Jetty, Cape Arago State Park, Boiler Bay State Scenic Viewpoint, or any place with a good view out over the ocean. Large flocks are commonly seen in August and September.

Mostly silent at sea.

Juvenile gulls are streaky and chunkier with broader wings that are set closer to the head.

LENGTH: 17.5" / WINGSPAN: 40"

Breeding adult.
White head, red bill, gray body, and a white border on the wings and tail.

Nonbreeding adult.
Smudged gray head. Young birds are dark brown.

HEERMANN'S GULL

Larus heermanni

The relationship between these eye-catching gulls and the pelicans they relentlessly follow and steal food from is known as kleptoparasitism. Heermann's Gulls and Brown Pelicans both nest on the Southern California coast, and when the Brown Pelicans fly north to Oregon after breeding, the gulls are never far behind.

Found over the ocean and in the lower parts of estuaries. Roosts on jetties and mudflats, often mixed with Brown Pelicans. Catches fish and invertebrates by swimming and diving, but also steals food.

Look for them at Fort Stevens State Park: South Jetty, Yaquina Bay South Jetty, and Umpqua River South Jetty. Uncommon to common June–November when they disperse northward after breeding.

Gives short barks and other single-note calls year-round.

Adult plumage and bill color are unique.

LENGTH: 19" / WINGSPAN: 51"

Nonbreeding adult.
Compact gull with dull
yellow legs and petite bill.
Round, smudged head
and dark eyes. Wings are
medium gray; wingtips are
black with large white spots.

First winter.
Mottled brown with a
little gray on the back.
Pink bill with black tip.

SHORT-BILLED GULL
(FORMERLY MEW GULL)

Larus brachyrhynchus

This delicate gull gathers by the thousands along the North Coast in late fall, scouring fields for beetles and worms. They associate with medium-sized gulls like Ring-billed and California Gulls.

Found in wet fields, on estuary mudflats, and around jetties. Feeds on insects, crustaceans, and fish. Bobs its head when walking.

Look for them at Wireless Road near Astoria, Brian Booth State Park, and Chetco Point Park. Common September–April.

Makes similar wails to other gulls, as well as single-note calls that are higher and shorter. Also makes a "pup-pup" call.

Similar species: see Ring-billed Gull entry page 155.

LENGTH: 16" / WINGSPAN: 43"

Nonbreeding adult.
Bright yellow legs and a relatively stubby yellow bill with a thick black ring. Eyes are pale yellow. Wings are very pale gray, and wingtips are black with a small white spot. Head has fine streaks.

First winter.
Whitish with a gray back and streaked brown wings with dark tips. Tail has a thick, dark band. Eyes are dark and bill is pink with a dark tip. Legs are pink.

RING-BILLED GULL

Larus delawarensis

This gull is mostly terrestrial, finding food on foot as it walks around fields and mudflats. They may be found mixed with smaller Short-billed Gulls in fields.

Found on beaches, estuaries, fields, and parking lots. Eats invertebrates, fish, grain, and garbage.

Look for them at Tillamook Bay Wetlands: Goodspeed Road, Yaquina Bay South Jetty, and the Gold Beach harbor. Common August–October, especially on the North Coast. Uncommon the rest of the year.

Makes similar wails, chuckles, barks, and grunts to those of the large gulls.

Similar species: see Short-billed Gull entry page 153 and California Gull entry page 157.

Nonbreeding adult.
Greenish yellow legs and a thin, yellow bill with both a red and a black spot. Wings medium gray; wingtips have extensive black with a small white spot. Brownish streaks on the nape.

First winter.
First-winter plumage is mottled brown all over with dark wingtips. Bill is pale pink with a dark tip.

CALIFORNIA GULL

Larus californicus

"Seagull" is a misnomer for these gulls, who begin their lives on rocky islands in lakes in the interior of the continent. They make large migratory movements along the coast, flying in tighter flocks than most gulls.

Found along the beach, flying over the ocean, and in fields. Eats fish, invertebrates, eggs, and garbage.

Look for them at Nehalem Bay State Park, Brian Booth State Park, and Rogue River South Jetty. Common July–November; uncommon otherwise.

Makes similar wails, chuckles, barks, and grunts to those of the large gulls.

Similar species: see Ring-billed Gull entry page 155 and Herring Gull entry page 159.

LENGTH: 21" / WINGSPAN: 54"

Nonbreeding adult.
Pale gray wings and pale eyes. Head is flattened with a sloped forehead. Medium yellow bill is long with a red spot and a slight bulge near the end. Legs are pink. Wingtips are black with a small white spot. Head and neck are heavily streaked.

First winter.
First- and second-winter plumages are similar: mottled brown with a dark tail. Bill is dark, becoming more pink in the second year.

Second or third winter.
Back is gray while wings are still mottled.

Nonbreeding adult Iceland Gull.
Smaller, greenish yellow bill, more rounded head, and dark eyes. Wingtips are pale below while Herring's are dark.

HERRING GULL

Larus argentatus

Many Herring Gulls spend the winter out on the ocean, appearing along the shore when winter storms push them east. Watch for the rarer Iceland Gull mixed in with their winter flocks.

Found along beaches and estuaries, in pastures, and in parking lots. Eats fish, crustaceans, and carrion. Mixes with flocks of other large gulls.

Look for them at D River Beach Wayside, Siuslaw River North Jetty, and Crissey Field State Park. Uncommon to common September–April, peaking October–December.

Large gulls make similar wails, chuckles, barks, and grunts. Long calls are given while tossing the head back and forward in a courtship display.

Iceland Gull is rare to uncommon October–April.

Adult.
Bulbous, bright yellow bill with a red spot. Wings are dark gray; wingtips are black with a little white. Head and neck are clean white.

Juvenile (left) and adult (right).
Juvenile and first-winter plumages are dark brownish gray with dark bills.

WESTERN GULL

Larus occidentalis

The full life cycle of this distinctive gull can be observed on the Oregon Coast: from spotted, fluffy nestling to begging juvenile to bright white-headed adult. Though their plumage is distinctive, they complicate identification by hybridizing with Glaucous-winged Gulls.

Found on beaches and docks, and in parking lots. Diet includes fish, invertebrates, carrion, eggs, and birds. Drops clams and cockles onto pavement or wet sand to break them open. Nests on offshore islands, cliffs, pilings, and bridges.

Look for them nesting at Haystack Rock near Cannon Beach, Yaquina Head Outstanding Natural Area, and Face Rock Wayside. Very common year-round.

Large gulls make similar wails, chuckles, barks, and grunts. Long calls are given while tossing the head back and forward in a courtship display. Young Western Gulls can be heard giving high pitched begging calls to adults long after they leave the nest.

Similar species: see Glaucous-winged Gull entry page 163.

LENGTH: 25" / WINGSPAN: 58"

Nonbreeding adult.
Large gull with gray wingtips and dark eye. Legs are pink. Large yellow bill with a red spot and a bulge at the end. Wings are medium gray; wingtips are darker gray and white. Head and neck are heavily smudged brownish gray.

Juvenile.
First- and second-winter plumages are pale brownish gray with dark bill.

Light juvenile Glaucous Gull.
Very large with white wingtips in all plumages. Often seen in juvenile plumage with a black-tipped pink bill.

GLAUCOUS-WINGED GULL

Larus glaucescens

This gull has the impressive and useful ability to detect paralytic shellfish poisoning in the bivalves it eats and regurgitate them before being poisoned. Hybridizes with Western, Herring, and Glaucous Gulls, producing a dizzying variety of intermediate plumages.

Found around beaches, bays, and rivers, and in flooded fields and parking lots. Feeds on fish and invertebrates and scavenges carrion and garbage. Nests on rock or sand islands.

Look for them in pastures around Tillamook, at Yachats State Park, and Rogue River South Jetty. Common year-round with a dip in summer.

Large gulls make similar wails, chuckles, barks, and grunts. Long calls are given while tossing the head back and forward in a courtship display.

Glaucous Gull is rare November–April. Similar species: see also Western Gull entry page 161.

Breeding adult.
Large tern with a heavy, red-orange bill. Adults have pale gray wings with dark tips below, black legs, and a black cap. Young birds may have a white forehead.

Nonbreeding adult Elegant Tern.
Smaller than Caspian, with a thinner, yellower bill.

CASPIAN TERN

Hydroprogne caspia

These acrobatic terns swoop and hover up to 100 feet in the air before diving down into the water to grab fish. At 10,000 terns, East Sand Island in the Columbia River Estuary is the largest Caspian Tern nesting colony in the world, hosting about two-thirds of the Pacific Coast population and around 10 percent of the world population.

Found flying over bays and the ocean. Roosts on sandbars, sometimes with gulls. Eats a variety of small fish, captured by diving. Nest is a depression in the sand on an island. Nests in large colonies but usually hunts alone.

Look for them at Fort Stevens State Park, Bayocean Peninsula, and Bullards Beach State Park. Common April–September on the North Coast. Uncommon on the South Coast.

Call is a harsh "kee-kareer" made in flight. In late summer, juveniles follow adults around and squeal at them.

Elegant Tern is rare to uncommon August–September. More frequent on South Coast.

LENGTH: 21" / WINGSPAN: 50"

Adult.
Large raptor-like bird with a bald, pink head. Plumage is brownish black with silvery flight feathers when seen from below. In flight, wings are held up in a V.

Immature.
Head is grayish.

TURKEY VULTURE

Cathartes aura

These waste management experts provide an important service: reducing disease by consuming carcasses. Vultures warm in the morning sun and wait for thermals (rising bodies of warm air) to form before they begin soaring in search of food.

Widespread over open country. Eats carrion, but also predates murre nests when adults are flushed. Likely nests near the coast, though documentation is scarce. Nests on cliffs or in an old stump or log. Roosts communally at night in trees and on structures. Often seen in groups, especially in migration or when circling a food source. Tips side to side when soaring.

Look for them at Nestucca Bay National Wildlife Refuge, Yaquina Head Outstanding Natural Area, and Cape Arago State Park. Common to very common March–September. Overwinters in low numbers on the South Coast.

Usually silent.

Hawks and eagles have feathered heads and are more stable when soaring.

Adult with fish.
Large raptor with crooked wings. Plumage is dark above and white below, with white and dark patches on the underwings.

Adult.
Dark stripe on the face and large, yellow eyes. Juveniles have buffy patches on the head and breast.

OSPREY

Pandion haliaetus

This fish-loving raptor happily uses artificial nesting platforms, allowing easy observation of its nesting behavior. The Osprey population has been growing, with the aid of these nesting platforms, since the pesticide DDT was outlawed in 1972.

Found hunting in rivers, estuaries, lakes, and the ocean near shore. Eats fish captured by diving from the air, feet first. Carries fish facing forward when flying. Builds stick nest on dead or broken-off trees, utility poles, or platforms.

Look for them at Knight County Park, Mark Hatfield Marine Science Center and Estuary Trail, and Coquille River jetties. Uncommon to common March–October. Winters in low numbers on the South Coast.

Gives calls in flight including a "tew" series and a gull-like scream.

Similar species: see Bald Eagle entry page 177.

LENGTH: 23" / WINGSPAN: 63"

Male.
Gray with a long tail, a white rump, and black on the wings. Wings held in a shallow V when gliding.

Female.
Adult females and juveniles of both sexes have brown wings and a white rump, but females have streaked chests and pale eyes while juveniles are orangish below with dark eyes.

Adult Cooper's Hawk.
Long, striped tail but lacks white rump patch. Does not fly slowly with wings held up in a V.

Adult Short-eared Owl.
Similar habitat and face shape but has a wider, paler face and buffy wing patches.

NORTHERN HARRIER

Circus hudsonius

The harrier's owllike face helps it hear rodents in the grass. They sometimes occupy the same habitat as Short-eared Owls and can engage in aerial fights around dusk when they are both hunting.

Found flying low over marshes and fields of tall grass. Hunts mammals and small birds, using sight and sound. Nests on the ground, hidden by grass. Performs aerial courtship displays that involve midair prey handoffs.

Look for them at Fort Stevens State Park, Mark Hatfield Marine Science Center and Estuary Trail, and Bandon Marsh National Wildlife Refuge. Rare to uncommon, with higher numbers in winter.

In alarm, males bark and females give a series of "keeks."

Short-eared Owl is rare. Cooper's Hawk is rare to uncommon.

Adult.
Orange breast and shoulders, black-and-white checkered wings, black-and-white banded tail.

Juvenile.
Streaky dark brown bib and less-defined wing and tail markings.

RED-SHOULDERED HAWK

Buteo lineatus

This inconspicuous raptor has recently and rapidly expanded its range northward up the Oregon Coast. They are more secretive than Red-tailed Hawks but their call is loud and distinctive.

Found in open lowlands and deciduous woodlands near water. Favors openings like farm fields and meadows. Eats a variety of small prey including mammals, birds, reptiles, amphibians, and crayfish. Constructs stick nest in a tree, often near water.

Look for them in fields around Tillamook, at Bandon Marsh National Wildlife Refuge, and Crissey Field State Park. Rare to uncommon on the North Coast. Uncommon to common on the South Coast.

Call is a fast, repeated series of hoarse "kleer" cries.

Similar species: see Red-tailed Hawk entry page 175.

Adult.
Reddish orange tail.

Juvenile.
All ages have a distinctive dark belly band. When perched, white spots on the shoulders form a V.

Juvenile.
Barred brown tail.

Light morph female Rough-legged Hawk.
Pale head, dark belly, and black wrist patches. Rough-leggeds frequently hover when hunting.

RED-TAILED HAWK

Buteo jamaicensis

This obliging hawk shows helpful field marks from every angle and often perches in plain sight near roads. It adapts well to human activities, like farming and logging, that create open areas for hunting.

Found in open areas like fields and roadsides. Hunts rodents, snakes, and other small animals from trees and utility poles. Makes a large stick nest high in a tree or on a cliff. Soars on thermals (rising bodies of warm air). Performs aerial courtship displays, diving and calling.

Look for them at Tillamook Bay Wetlands: Goodspeed Road, Beaver Creek State Natural Area, and Bandon Marsh National Wildlife Refuge. Uncommon to common. More are present in the winter.

Their harsh scream is an iconic sound used in many movies set in the West.

Rough-legged Hawk is rare. Similar species: see also Red-shouldered Hawk entry page 173.

Adult. Very large raptor with large head and bill. Wings are broad and straight. Feet are large and yellow.

Female birds of prey are often larger than males. The female Bald Eagle is on the left.

Immature. Bald Eagle plumage changes over the first four to five years but is always a mix of mottled white and dark brown. Bill starts out dark and gets yellower with age.

Adult Golden Eagle. Lacks the white mottling of a young Bald Eagle and has a golden nape.

BALD EAGLE

Haliaeetus leucocephalus

Once decimated by deadly pesticides concentrated in its food items, this adaptable bird of prey has returned in large numbers to Oregon. Expanded eagle populations are now predating murres and other birds.

Found all along the coast where they hunt in both freshwater and saltwater. Perches in tall trees and lands on beaches to consume prey. Hunts fish, seabirds, and waterfowl, and scavenges dead animals and the placentas of seals. Nests in forested areas where it makes huge stick nests in large trees.

Look for them at Nestucca Bay National Wildlife Refuge, Yaquina Head Outstanding Natural Area, and Cape Arago State Park. Common to very common year-round with a dip in the fall when they move north to feed on salmon runs.

Gives a series of screams and a fast "kee" series. Sounds are high-pitched for such a large bird.

Golden Eagle is rare at the coast.

Male.
Rufous back, blue-gray wings, and a rufous tail with a black band.

Female.
Reddish brown with black barring on the wings, tail, and back. Both sexes have bold markings on the head.

Adult Merlin.
Slightly larger and bulkier and lacks any rusty color. Facial markings are more subtle.

AMERICAN KESTREL

Falco sparverius

The smallest falcon in North America has a petite head and bill that give it an endearing appearance, but it is still a formidable predator. Kestrels hover while holding their heads stationary to spot their prey.

Found in open fields, meadows, and roadsides. Perches on power lines, making it easy to spot, even at highway speeds. Not found on the outer coast, but present just inland in open fields. Eats insects like grasshoppers, and hunts rodents and small birds as well. Nests in tree cavities made by woodpeckers, but also uses nest boxes.

Look for them in fields around Tillamook, at Nestucca Bay National Wildlife Refuge, and Cape Blanco State Park. Common November–February; rare otherwise.

A series of "klee, klee, klee" calls.

Merlin is uncommon September–April.

Adult.
Dark cheeks and cap produce a helmeted look. Dark gray back and dark horizontal barring across the belly. Looks large and powerful in flight.

Juvenile.
Dark brown back and dark streaks below.

PEREGRINE FALCON

Falco peregrinus

An awe-inspiring sight cruising along coastal cliffs and diving through the air to hunt birds. Peregrines also take to the air to perform courtship displays and chase other raptors out of their territories.

Hunts along bays, mudflats, beaches, rocky shores, and over the ocean, wherever there are birds to hunt and room to build up speed. Primarily preys on birds, including ducks, gulls, seabirds, shorebirds, and songbirds. Often captures prey in a high-speed dive, called a stoop, at over 200 miles per hour. Nest is a scrape on an elevated rock ledge.

Look for nesting birds at Cape Meares State Park and Yaquina Head Outstanding Natural Area. Uncommon year-round. Individuals are found near nesting sites throughout the year.

Emits a series of screams and screeches, especially in the spring and near the nest.

Similar species: see the much smaller Merlin on page 178.

Adult.
Large and gray, with yellow bill and legs. Plumage has purplish tones. White collar on nape with iridescent green below. Tail has a wide, pale gray band.

Adult Rock Pigeon.
Variable plumage but has pink legs and a dark bill.

Adult Eurasian Collared-Dove.
Pale beige and gray with a black collar. Tail is long with white edges.

BAND-TAILED PIGEON

Patagioenas fasciata

This colorful frugivore roams the forest to take advantage of the seasonal bounty. Band-tails travel up to 30 miles from their nest to find ripe berries.

Found in conifer forests but also visits feeders and farms for seeds and grain. Builds a stick nest in a tree. Most visible when moving in small flocks or gathering at mineral sites to consume clay for digestion. Also seen perching atop tall trees.

Look for them at Nestucca Bay National Wildlife Refuge, Siltcoos River: Waxmyrtle Trail, and Arizona Beach State Recreation Site. Uncommon to common March–October; rare otherwise.

Male sings repeated "hip WOO, hip WOO" from the top of a tree. Listening in the morning can be the best way to find one.

Rock Pigeon and Eurasian Collared-Dove are introduced species that are common year-round near houses and farms.

LENGTH: 14.5" / WINGSPAN: 26"

Male.
Stocky with a large head and sharp bill. Single bluish band across a white breast. All plumages are blue-gray above with a shaggy, crownlike crest.

Female.
Rufous belly band and sides in addition to the blue band. Juveniles have a dark breast-band with rufous sides.

BELTED KINGFISHER

Megaceryle alcyon

A boisterous bird whose apt name describes both its appearance and its diet. Its spiky crown and fish-stabbing bill give it a comical, memorable look.

Found in fresh and saltwater, in bays, rivers, creeks, ponds, wetlands, and tidal marshes. Uses trees, snags, wires, and pilings as perches from which to dive for food. Primarily consumes fish but also takes crustaceans and mollusks. Digs a nest burrow into vertical stream banks. Noisy and active, this bird is easily detected when present.

Look for them at Necanicum River Estuary, Sitka Sedge State Natural Area, and Siltcoos River: Waxmyrtle Trail. Common year-round though less detectable during the summer nesting season.

Very vocal. Makes loud rattles, both a slow and a fast version, that carry across the water.

Plumage color, shape, and behavior are unique.

Male.
Red spot on back of head.
Juveniles show red spot
on front of the crown
during their first summer.

Female.
Tiny with a short bill that
emerges from fuzzy feathers.
Tail black with white edges
and black spots.

DOWNY WOODPECKER

Dryobates pubescens

Acting more like a chickadee, our smallest woodpecker is active and noisy as it forages on slender trunks and branches. Forms wintertime mixed flocks with chickadees, kinglets, and creepers.

Found in deciduous forests and woodlands and in developed areas. Pecks on branches and tree trunks to find invertebrates. Also eats fruit occasionally. Excavates nest cavities in dead tree trunks or limbs.

Look for them at Cannon Beach Settling Ponds, Beaver Creek State Natural Area, and Arizona Beach State Recreation Site. Common year-round.

Makes a "pik" call and also strings the "piks" together into a whinny. Vocalizes frequently.

Similar species: see Hairy Woodpecker entry page 189.

LENGTH: 6.75" / WINGSPAN: 12"

Male.
Red spot on back of head.
Juveniles show a red spot
on the front of the crown
during their first summer.

Female.
Medium sized with a
long bill. Tail is black
with white edges.

HAIRY WOODPECKER

Dryobates villosus

The larger of two similar woodpecker species and the one that looks like it would be scary to hold. Downy Woodpeckers have petite bills, but Hairys have bills as long as their heads.

Found in all forest types, but especially conifers. Prefers larger trees. Also uses burned forests. Eats primarily insects (especially beetles) and spiders with a small amount of plant matter. Pecks holes in trees and removes bark to find prey. Excavates nest cavities in dead trees. Drums on trees to advertise its territory.

Look for them at Oswald West State Park, Nestucca Bay National Wildlife Refuge, and Harris Beach State Park. Uncommon to common year-round.

Call is a loud "peek." Also gives a rattle that is harsher than the Downy Woodpecker's whinny.

Similar species: see Downy Woodpecker entry page 187.

Male.
Large, brownish, with a long bill and a red mustache. Black spots and shield on breast. Back is brown with black barring. Rump is white and very visible in flight. Bright red-orange feathers on underside of wings and tail.

Female.
Same overall look as male, but without a red mustache.

NORTHERN FLICKER

Colaptes auratus

The ground might seem like a strange place to see a wood-pecker, but flickers go where the ants are. They can also be seen on trees or utility poles performing stylized dance-offs that may serve a pair bonding purpose.

Found in neighborhoods, in open woodlands, and along forest edges. Eats ants, other invertebrates, berries, and nuts. Excavates nest cavities in dead and decaying trees. Chooses exposed perches high in trees, unlike other woodpeckers.

Look for them at Fort Stevens State Park, Beaver Creek State Natural Area, and Bullards Beach State Park. Common to very common year-round.

Noisy, especially in spring. Drums rapidly on metal sur-faces for a louder sound. In spring, gives a fast "keek" series, often with drumming. Other common calls include a single plaintive "kleer" and a "wik-a wik-a" series.

The pattern and brownish color of their plumage are dis-tinct among the local woodpeckers.

LENGTH: 12.5" / WINGSPAN: 20"

Adult.
Black head and back, and a crest that it can raise and lower. Deep blue plumage with black barring on wings and tail.

Adult California Scrub-Jay.
Wings and tail are blue, back is gray. Underparts are dingy white with a thin blue breast-band. Tail is long and hangs down when perching

STELLER'S JAY

Cyanocitta stelleri

If you think you hear a hawk calling, make sure it isn't really this noisy forest dweller. Steller's Jays are excellent mimics and often make hawk and eagle calls.

Found in conifer and conifer-deciduous forests. Eats a wide variety of foods including fruits, seeds, insects, and the eggs and young of other birds. Makes a bulky stick nest in a tree. Hops on the ground and jumps between tree branches. Quieter and more secretive during breeding season.

Look for them at Fort Stevens State Park, Cape Perpetua, and Humbug Mountain State Park. Very common year-round and easily found by ear.

Loud and raspy vocalist, with many different calls. Most common are a chuckle that is a rapid series of "shek" sounds, a harsh "snarl," and a quiet chatter.

California Scrub-Jay is uncommon to common year-round, especially in coastal towns.`

LENGTH: 11.5" / WINGSPAN: 19"

Adult.
Black plumage, legs, and
bill. Juveniles have blue eyes
and pink skin, called a gape,
at the corner of the bill.

AMERICAN CROW

Corvus brachyrhynchos

One of the most commonly seen birds at the coast, crows thrive in human-altered areas and tolerate human activity but are rarer in forests and "wilder" areas where ravens are more common.

Found in a wide variety of habitats. Omnivorous, it eats nuts, berries, small animals, eggs, clams, roadkill, and garbage. Also digs up mole crabs and eats their eggs, leaving the crabs behind. Nest is a mass of sticks and bark on a tree branch. Chases and mobs ravens and birds of prey.

Look for them almost everywhere at the coast, with higher numbers in areas with more human activity. Very common year-round, especially in areas inhabited by people.

In addition to their well-known nasal "caw," they also emit gurgles, groans, and rattles.

Similar species: see Common Raven entry page 197.

LENGTH: 17.5" / WINGSPAN: 39"

Adult.
Very large corvid, glossy black with a heavy bill. Long throat feathers blow in the wind. Juveniles have blue eyes and pink skin, called a gape, at the corner of the bill.

Adult.
Ravens have wedge-shaped tails with longer central feathers.

COMMON RAVEN

Corvus corax

Our largest songbirds, ravens are known for their intelligence as well as their vocal capabilities. They exhibit many interesting behaviors, and you may get to watch them caching food, having social interactions, or performing barrel rolls in the sky.

Found along beaches and roads and in fields and forest openings. Less common in towns than crows. Eats small animals, eggs, and insects, and scavenges carrion. Makes stick nests in large trees or on rocky outcroppings, away from disturbance. Locomotion includes both walking and hopping, and it soars more than crows do.

Look for them at Oswald West State Park, Cape Perpetua, and Harris Beach State Park. Common year-round.

Voice is deep and hoarse. Calls are varied and include caws, croaks, screams, rattles, and honks. Often calls in flight.

Similar species: see American Crow entry page 195.

LENGTH: 24" / WINGSPAN: 53"

Male.
Green with grayish chest and an iridescent magenta gorget that covers the crown and throat.

Female.
Green and gray with a small patch of reddish feathers on the throat. Juveniles are grayer with shorter bills, no red on throat.

ANNA'S HUMMINGBIRD

Calypte anna

The only year-round hummingbird in the Pacific Northwest survives winter by lowering its body temperature at night. Anna's Hummingbirds have expanded their range dramatically northward with the help of humans and the flowers and feeders that they provide.

Found in towns and open woodlands. Drinks nectar from flowers and bird feeders and eats small insects and spiders. Also drinks from sap wells made by sapsuckers. Nest is a tiny cup made of lichens, cattail fluff, and other plant materials and held together by spiderwebs.

Look for them at Salishan Nature Trail, Yachats Commons Park, and Harris Beach State Park. Common to very common year-round.

Song is a series of high, scratchy sounds, given any time of year. Dive display produces a loud "hee." Both sexes make a chitter sound during aggression. Sharp "chip" calls are commonly heard.

Similar species: see Rufous Hummingbird entry page 201.

Male.
Rufous with some green on
the back and head possible.
Gorget is coppery orange.

Female.
Greener with rufous
on the sides and tail.

Male Allen's Hummingbird.
Often greener than Rufous
Hummingbird, but they
frequently hybridize.

RUFOUS HUMMINGBIRD

Selasphorus rufus

These fiery little birds arrive in spring from as far south as Mexico and aggressively defend their food sources. A male's displays include a swooping dive and a horizontal shuttle between two points.

Found in a variety of habitats. Eats small insects and feeds on flower nectar and at feeders. Nests in wooded areas with understory plants. Female builds a tiny nest out of moss and lichen adhered with spiderwebs.

Look for them at Alder Creek Farm in Manzanita, Nestucca Bay National Wildlife Refuge, and Silt-coos River: Waxmyrtle Trail. Migrants begin to arrive in mid-February and peak in April. Common until they depart in September.

Vocalization is a fast, buzzy "dzeet-chippity." Chip call is given by both sexes. Male's wings make a metallic trill in flight.

Allen's Hummingbird hybridizes with Rufous Hummingbird on the South Coast to such an extent that few birds there are likely to be pure Allen's or Rufous. Identification requires a very good look at the shape of tail feathers.

LENGTH: 3.75" / WINGSPAN: 4.5"

Male.
Glossy blue-black body
with black wings. Long,
pointed wings, notched tail.

Female.
Dark above and pale gray on
the belly, collar, and forehead.

Adult Northern Rough-winged Swallow.
Somewhat resembles a female martin
but is smaller, warmer brown, and
lacks the pale collar and forehead.

Adult Vaux's Swift.
Plumage is uniform gray.
Tail is short. Leading
edge of the wings is
rounded, with no visible
joint. Quickly flutters
wings instead of flapping.

PURPLE MARTIN

Progne subis

Our largest swallow sounds like a bird-robot hybrid spreading techno music through the skies. Loss of snags, standing dead trees, means that martins rely heavily on human-made nest cavities, which require maintenance and management for best results.

Feeds on aerial insects, especially large ones, over open areas and forests. Nests colonially in cavities in snags or in nest boxes or gourds located in open areas. Faces nest-site competition from introduced European Starlings and House Sparrows.

Look for them at Netarts Bay Boat Basin, Mark Hatfield Marine Science Center and Estuary Trail, and Salmon Harbor Marina. Uncommon April–September.

Vocal in flight. Song is complex, with trills and "tews" and "burrts." Most common call is a burry "veer."

Northern Rough-winged Swallow is uncommon April–August. Vaux's Swift is uncommon April–September.

Male.
Glossy blue-green with dark wings and a bright white belly. Dark face with a white chin.

Female.
Dark gray above and white below.

Adult Bank Swallow.
Dark breastband. Pale gray back contrasts with its wings.

TREE SWALLOW

Tachycineta bicolor

This feisty swallow's metallic blue back is the color of the ocean on a sunny summer day. Named for their habit of nesting in tree cavities, they also readily use nest boxes.

Found flying in open areas near water. Picks small insects from the air, the water, and vegetation. Also eats fruit when insects are scarce. Loud at the nest cavity, chasing away intruders.

Look for them at Astoria Mitigation Bank Wetlands, Beaver Creek State Natural Area, and Bandon Marsh National Wildlife Refuge. Uncommon to common March–September.

Song consists of slurred whistles and chirps. Call is a repeated "cheet."

Bank Swallow is rare at the coast. Similar species: see also Violet-green Swallow entry page 207.

LENGTH: 5.75" / WINGSPAN: 14.5"

Male.
Green and violet on the wings and violet on the rump. White flanks wrap up onto the sides of the rump. Face is white above the eye.

Female.
Gray above. Face is smudged gray but may have a little white above the eye.

VIOLET-GREEN SWALLOW

Tachycineta thalassina

These colorful swallows sound like they are battling with ray guns as they swoop and dive. They forage higher in the air than other swallows and are less likely to be down at eye level.

Hunts for insects over forests and higher elevation areas. Nests in cavities made by woodpeckers or in nest boxes. Roosts in large numbers on power lines during migration.

Look for them at Ecola State Park, Cape Perpetua, and Humbug Mountain State Park. Common March–September.

Calls include a monotone "cheet" and squeaky "chwee." Song is similar to the call.

Similar species: see Tree Swallow entry page 205.

Male.
Dark, glossy blue above with orange-red throat. Males have an orange belly and a longer forked tail than females. Females are paler below.

BARN SWALLOW

Hirundo rustica

This swallow lives up to its name, nesting on all kinds of human-made structures, apparently unbothered by people and livestock. It also frequents parks and beaches, offering eye-level views of its beautiful plumage.

Forages for aerial insects over fields, beaches, and water. Nest is a cup made from mud and grass attached to the wall of a human-made structure. Gathers in large night-time roosts during migration.

Look for them at Sunset Beach Recreation Area, Siuslaw River South Jetty, and Chetco Point Park. Common April–September.

Song, often given in flight, is a fast, long collection of notes and trills. Makes a variety of noisy calls including a high "squeep" and a polyphonic "jit."

Similar species: see Cliff Swallow entry page 211.

LENGTH: 6.75" / WINGSPAN: 15"

Adult.
Wings and tail are dark brown, underparts are pale, and rump is buffy.

Adult in the nest.
Red cheek and throat, distinctive pale "headlight" on forehead.

CLIFF SWALLOW

Petrochelidon pyrrhonota

Cliff Swallows do everything in groups, whether nesting or foraging. They give special calls to alert members of their colony to the presence of danger or clouds of insects.

Found foraging for aerial insects in open areas. Nests colonially, constructing gourd-shaped mud nests on the sheltered walls of buildings, overpasses, and cliffs. Can be seen gathering mud from puddles and the edges of wetlands with their wings held up to stay clean.

Look for them at Wireless Road near Astoria, Dean Creek Elk Viewing Area, and Arizona Beach State Recreation Site. Uncommon April–August.

Song is long and full of squeaks and ticks. Calls include harsh "churts" and slurred "zeers."

Similar species: see Barn Swallow entry page 209.

Adult.
Gray back, white cheek on a black face. Flanks are buffy, belly is white. Bill is small.

BLACK-CAPPED CHICKADEE

Poecile atricapillus

This small but feisty bird puts up a loud fuss when it spies a potential threat, whether it be owl, hawk, or cat. Chickadees form mixed flocks in winter with other bird species and vocally mob predators together.

Found in deciduous and mixed forests, wetlands, and neighborhoods. Eats insects, seeds, and fruits obtained by perching, hovering, or hanging from twigs. Common feeder bird. Excavates a nest cavity in a partially rotten snag or branch. Also uses nest boxes.

Look for them at Cannon Beach Settling Ponds, Salishan Nature Trail, and Millicoma Marsh. Common year-round.

Very vocal. Song is a whistled "fee-bee" or "bee-bee-bee-bee." Also makes a musical "gurgle" song. Call is a "chick-a-dee" with discernible syllables. "Seet" calls are given in alarm.

Similar species: see Chestnut-backed Chickadee entry page 215.

Adult.
Tiny bird with a warm
brown back and flanks.
White cheek on a black
face. Bill is tiny.

CHESTNUT-BACKED CHICKADEE

Poecile rufescens

This denizen of conifer forests is often heard high in the canopy, calling as it flits from branch to branch. Near forested areas they visit feeders and will use nest boxes.

Prefers large, continuous areas of conifer forest. Feeds in the tree canopy where it hovers and hangs from twigs to grab insects. Uses woodpecker cavities for nesting or excavates a cavity in snags or dead branches.

Look for them at Cape Meares State Park, Mike Miller County Park, and Humbug Mountain State Park. Common year-round.

Song is a warbled gurgle. Calls include a short, high-pitched, buzzy "chick-a-dee" and a fast "seet" series.

Similar species: see Black-capped Chickadee entry page 213. Golden-crowned Kinglet (page 219) sounds similar and inhabits similar environments.

Adult.
Pale iris and small, pale eyebrow. Breast is peachy and streaked.

Female Bushtit.
Much smaller than Wrentit, has a tiny bill, and is often found in flocks.

WRENTIT

Chamaea fasciata

A floppy-tailed gray-brown bird whose secretive habits often lead to obstructed views. The Wrentit is an emblematic bird of coastal chaparral whose loud song alerts you to its skulking presence.

Found in coastal chaparral habitats and other dense brush like huckleberry, salal, Nootka rose, blackberry, and willow. Also found in clear-cuts. Eats invertebrates and berries. Nest is a cup located low and deep in a bush.

Look for them at Bayocean Peninsula, Siltcoos River: Waxmyrtle Trail, and Harris Beach State Park. More common on the South Coast. Present year-round.

Male song is an accelerating series of "pip" notes, ending in a trill. Tempo is reminiscent of a bouncing ball. Female song is a series of chirps. Alarm call is a harsh chatter.

Bushtit is uncommon year-round.

Adult.
Grayish green overall with greenish
yellow on wings and a white wing bar.
Yellow-orange crest edged in black
and underlined by a white eyebrow
and dark smudge through the eye.

GOLDEN-CROWNED KINGLET

Regulus satrapa

These tiny forest sprites flutter from tree to tree in the heights of the canopy, singing at the upper edge of human hearing. Kinglets are constantly in motion, hovering to glean insects from conifer branches and clusters of lichen.

Prefers older conifer forests for breeding but is more flexible with habitat choice in winter. Forages high in trees in summer, but often feeds in lower vegetation in cold weather. Flocks huddle together for warmth on cold nights.

Look for them at Ecola State Park, Cape Meares State Park, and Cape Blanco State Park. Common year-round.

Song is a series of high-pitched, accelerating notes. The final notes are reminiscent of Chestnut-backed Chickadee. Calls are a high "psip" or "seet," and they call softly and frequently to each other as they forage.

Similar species: see Ruby-crowned Kinglet entry page 221. Chestnut-backed Chickadee (page 215) sounds similar and inhabits similar environments.

Male.
Small olive-yellow bird with a white eyering. May show his red crown. Dark legs and yellow feet.

Adult Hutton's Vireo.
Similar plumage but is larger and chunkier with a thicker bill and gray feet.

RUBY-CROWNED KINGLET

Corthylio calendula

Hyperactive and loud, these little songbirds make their presence known. Males raise their red crowns during courtship and conflicts and lower them when foraging.

Found in a variety of habitats with trees and bushes. Usually seen feeding near eye level. Active feeders, constantly hopping and fluttering to scour every surface of leaves and twigs. Primarily feeds on a variety of arthropods but may also eat seeds or fruit. Joins mixed-species flocks in winter with chickadees, nuthatches, wrens, and Golden-crowned Kinglets.

Look for them at Clay Myers State Natural Area, Mike Miller County Park, and Bullards Beach State Park. Common September–May.

Song is a complex series that includes whistles, couplets, and triplets. Song is often heard in migration, away from breeding grounds. Call is frequently given during foraging, a hard "jit" or "jiddit."

Hutton's Vireo is uncommon year-round. Similar species: see also Golden-crowned Kinglet entry page 219.

LENGTH: 4.25" / WINGSPAN: 7.5"

Adult.
Grayish above, pale
below, yellowish sides.
Pale face gives it a "cute"
look. Bill is chunky.

WARBLING VIREO

Vireo gilvus

This cryptic bird might remain undetected in the shadows of the tree canopy if it weren't for its loud, frequent singing. Warbling Vireos forage high up in deciduous trees, but during migration can be found feeding at eye level.

Found in areas of deciduous trees and shrubs. Active like warblers, fluttering to grab prey including caterpillars and beetles. Nest is a cup woven from bark and grass that hangs below a *V* of twigs in a tree.

Look for them at Cannon Beach Settling Ponds, Brian Booth State Park, and Crissey Field State Park. Uncommon to common late April–September with a peak May–June.

Call is a "jit" or a harsh whine. Song is a slow, burry warble with many phrases, jumping between high and low tones. One mnemonic is "cheeseburger, cheeseburger, cheese." Males may sing from the nest.

Lack of eyering or spectacles separates it from the other local vireos.

Adult.
Small olive-yellow flycatcher with a thick, teardrop-shaped eyering. Pale wingbars. Wingtips do not extend far beyond the base of the tail.

Adult Hammond's Flycatcher.
Grayer with a smaller bill, longer wingtips, and a less prominent eyering.

PACIFIC-SLOPE FLYCATCHER

Empidonax difficilis

The genus *Empidonax* is represented by several flycatcher species in Oregon, but the Pacific-slope is the most abundant at the coast. The challenge of identifying all of these small flycatchers is a fun puzzle for experienced birders.

Found in coniferous and deciduous forests and prefers areas near water and older stands of trees. Eats insects caught in the air. Nests in tree cavities, tree branches, behind loose bark, and in the roots of fallen trees. Sings from high in the canopy.

Look for them at Ecola State Park, Cape Perpetua, and South Slough National Estuarine Research Reserve. Common to very common May–July. Becomes quieter in August and departs by September.

Song is made up of three phrases that can be sung in any order: "psee-bit!...chi-peet!...teet!" Calls include a rising "pseweet" and a "tink."

Hammond's Flycatcher is uncommon April–September but more prevalent in the Coast Range.

LENGTH: 5.5" / WINGSPAN: 8"

Adult.
Gray-black above
with a white belly
and undertail. Head
has a slight crest. Bill
is thin and black.

Adult Say's Phoebe.
Drab gray-brown with
a peachy belly.

BLACK PHOEBE

Sayornis nigricans

A recent and welcome addition to the bird fauna of the Oregon Coast, Black Phoebes have quickly and dramatically expanded their range up the coast over the last 20 years.

Attracted to the hunting perches and nesting substrates provided by human environments like farms. Prefers areas near still or slow water including creeks, ponds, canals, and wetlands. Hunts in open areas with low perches from which it flies out to catch insects in the air or drops to the ground. Makes a nest from mud and plant material on a bridge or a building.

Look for them at Cannon Beach Settling Ponds, Millicoma Marsh, and Chetco Point Park. Uncommon to common year-round.

Calls frequently. "Tew" and "teer" calls can be heard all year. Male sings a quick "pi-teer, pibreer."

Say's Phoebe is rare along the coast.

LENGTH: 7" / WINGSPAN: 11"

Adult.
Tiny brown wren with a
stubby tail held straight up.
Plumage is subtly barred
in shades of brown with a
paler eyebrow. Pointed bill.

Adult House Wren.
Grayer and paler than
Pacific Wren. Found
in deciduous for-
ests and clear-cuts.

PACIFIC WREN

Troglodytes pacificus

This mouselike bird sings its sweet song from the mossy, fern-covered forest floor. Pacific Wrens also call frequently and are vocally responsive to disturbance by people or potential predators.

Found in moist conifer forests with large woody debris and understory vegetation. May disperse in winter to parks and deciduous forest patches. Forages near the ground and chooses low perches to sing. Eats invertebrates including beetles, spiders, and caterpillars. Nests in cavities or under logs and vegetation.

Look for them at Ecola State Park, Mike Miller County Park, and Humbug Mountain State Park. Common year-round, though quieter outside of breeding season.

Very long, continuous song of varied warbles and trills lasting 5–30 seconds. Call is a harsh "jit," often repeated. It sings year-round, a welcome sound in the dead of winter.

House Wren is rare along the coast but can be found in clear-cuts in the Coast Range April–August.

Adult.
Pale eyebrow below a brown cap, and a long, pointed bill. Reddish shoulders and rump are distinctive. Barred wings and tail. Tail held cocked up.

MARSH WREN

Cistothorus palustris

Singing from amid the cattails, they provide the soundtrack of summer in a wetland. Despite their abundance and noisiness, it can be hard to get a good view of one because they so rarely perch in the open.

As the name suggests, occupies wetland vegetation including cattails, rushes, and introduced reed canary grass. Feeds on a wide variety of invertebrates found near the water and in vegetation. Nest is a domed basket woven in marsh vegetation over water.

Look for them at Astoria Mitigation Bank Wetlands, Sitka Sedge State Natural Area, and Bandon Marsh National Wildlife Refuge. Common year-round, though less detectable outside breeding season.

Song begins with "tick" notes then goes into a complex trill. Call is a harsh "chit." Song and call are loud and frequent.

Similar species: see Bewick's Wren entry page 233.

Adult.
Warm brown above and pale gray below, with a crisp white eyebrow. Often holds its barred tail up.

BEWICK'S WREN

Thryomanes bewickii

Very vocal birds that thrive in the brushy edges of human environments. Brambles like Himalayan blackberry and Nootka rose offer them the shelter and protection that they prefer.

Occupies a wide variety of shrubby habitats, from brushy clear-cuts and open forests to parks and neighborhoods. Slinks along trees, woody debris, and on the ground to find insect and spider prey. Makes a cup nest in a cavity or on a ledge, sometimes using human structures. Males sing from exposed perches.

Look for them in areas with a mix of thick bushes and open space. Common year-round.

Their short song consists of a few single notes followed by a trill. The long song has buzzes and more single notes. Calls include snarls, chitters, and other buzzy sounds.

Similar species: see Marsh Wren entry page 231.

Male.
Slate gray back and wings with orange wing-bars. Orange eyebrow and a dark breastband.

Female.
Similar plumage pattern to male's but in gray-brown and yellow-orange tones.

VARIED THRUSH

Ixoreus naevius

Spooky calls and a flash of orange in the spruce trees are sometimes the only signs of this resident of moist forests. Varied Thrushes often flush up into a tree if disturbed while foraging on the ground.

Prefers mature conifer forest, especially old growth, during the breeding season. In winter, occupies low-elevation forests and can be seen foraging along paths and roads. Eats a variety of invertebrates as well as berries.

Look for them at Oswald West State Park, Cape Perpetua, and Honeyman State Park. Common in winter and rare in summer.

Song is a lingering polyphonic whistle where multiple notes are sung simultaneously. Alarm call is a "chup." Begins singing early in spring, or even in winter.

Similar species: see American Robin entry page 239.

Adult.
Sparrow sized with a warm brown back, wings, and tail. Thin, buffy eyering. Breast is buffy with dark spots.

Adult Hermit Thrush.
Very similar to Swainson's but has rufous on the tail and darker spots on the breast. Frequently flicks its wings.

SWAINSON'S THRUSH

Catharus ustulatus

Each spring they arrive in large numbers and fill the forests with their ethereal songs. Swainson's Thrushes are often hidden but vocal—you might hear a dozen for every one you see.

Found in conifer forests, especially those near streams and with understory vegetation. Eats fruits like elderberries and salmonberries. Also feeds on arthropods like beetles and ants. Builds a cup nest in a bush or small tree.

Look for them at Nestucca Bay National Wildlife Refuge, South Slough National Estuarine Research Reserve, and Harris Beach State Park. Common to very common May–July. Quieter in August and September.

Song is a series of polyphonic notes that spirals upward, flutelike. Most songs are heard at dusk and dawn or on cloudy days. Calls include a "pwut" that sounds like a water drop, a braying "wee-churr," and a whistled "wee."

Swainson's is a coastal breeder and Hermit Thrush spends the winter, but they may overlap during migration.

LENGTH: 7" / WINGSPAN: 12"

Adult.
Distinctive red-orange breast, white
arcs around the eyes, yellow bill.
Juveniles have spotted underparts.

AMERICAN ROBIN

Turdus migratorius

The mild winters and lush fields and forests of the coast provide a haven for robins. Robin song is one of the earliest parts of the spring dawn chorus, starting well before the sun rises.

Found in pastures, lawns, and roadsides. Thrives in areas of human development, eating worms from lawns and fruit from ornamental trees. Robins find worms by sight and can be seen cocking their heads for a better view. Nest is a grassy cup held together with mud and located in a tree or bush or on a human structure.

Look for them in fields and forests as well as towns. Very common year-round with peak abundance in spring.

Song is a slow series of phrases: "Cheerio, cheerily, cheery-up." May add a "hissely" at the end. Gives a quick whinny of "cheep" or "kuk" notes. Calls include "squee-squeep," "tseerp," and "seet."

Juvenile robins could be confused with spotted thrushes like Swainson's but are larger and grayer. Adults are unmistakable.

LENGTH: 10" / WINGSPAN: 17"

Adult.
Smooth brown with soft crest and black mask, edged in white. Yellow belly. Tail has yellow tip, and some wing feathers have red, waxy tips.

Juvenile.
Grayish with streaks on the breast and more white on face.

CEDAR WAXWING

Bombycilla cedrorum

These gregarious birds are named for the red wax on their wings that may be a signal to potential mates. They gather in large flocks in the nonbreeding season, but can be seen in groups any time of year.

Found in woodlands, areas near streams, parks, and neighborhoods. Eats berries and insects. Flies out from a perch like a flycatcher to catch insects midair. Nest is a cup built in a tree or bush.

Look for them at Circle Creek Conservation Area, Salishan Nature Trail, and Arizona Beach State Recreation Site. Common May–October; rare otherwise.

Makes a high, thin, whistled "seet" and a high trill.

The combination of brownish plumage, yellow tail tip, and crest are unique among birds in western Oregon.

Male.
Red eyebrow, throat, breast, and rump. Curved culmen (upper part of the bill). Flanks have brownish streaks.

Female.
Brown overall with indistinct facial markings and brownish streaks on breast and flanks.

HOUSE FINCH

Haemorhous mexicanus

This quintessential backyard bird makes great use of yards: visiting feeders, munching on plants, and sometimes nesting on houses. It celebrates the first signs of spring by chowing down on the buds and flowers of decorative cherry trees.

Found in open deciduous woodlands, neighborhoods, and agricultural areas. Eats almost entirely plant matter including seeds, fruits, blossoms, and leaves. Forages on the ground or in plants. Nest is a cup placed in a tree or bush or on a structure.

Look for them at Sunset Beach Recreation Area, Yaquina Bay State Park, and Millicoma Marsh. Common year-round.

Song is a musical warble. Calls include a slurred "zree" and varied chirps.

Similar species: see Purple Finch entry page 245.

Male.
Washed all over
with purplish
pink. Bill is thick.

Female.
Olive-brown with thick,
blurry streaks below. Dis-
tinct brown ear patch, off-
set by paler areas.

PURPLE FINCH

Haemorhous purpureus

This sweetly singing finch gets its name from the raspberry-juice hue of its plumage. Purple Finches are the "wilder" cousins of House Finches, preferring forested habitats to backyards.

Breeds in conifer and mixed forests and along forest edges. After breeding, moves to areas with berries. Winters in woodlands, brushy areas, and neighborhoods. Eats a wide variety of plant matter and a few insects. Nest is a cup built in a tree.

Look for them at Nehalem Bay State Park, Beaver Creek State Natural Area, and Lone Ranch State Wayside. Common April–July; rare to uncommon otherwise.

Song is a sweet, bubbly warble. May also sing burry, disjointed phrases like a vireo. Calls include a slurred "weew" and a spitting "pwik."

Similar species: see House Finch entry page 243.

Male.
Red with dark wings.
Large-headed look.
Bill is curved, top and
bottom mandibles cross.

Female.
Females and first-year birds
are yellow with dark wings.

Juvenile.
Streaky brown and
may have wingbars.

RED CROSSBILL

Loxia curvirostra

The Oregon Coast is home to several Red Crossbill "types," differentiated by their calls and preferred conifer species. They use their distinctive crossed bills to pry open spruce and fir cones and eat the seeds.

Moves around conifer forests to find large cone crops. Also feeds on alder and birch cones. Nest is a cup built in a conifer tree. Often seen in flocks at the tops of conifer trees where cones are most plentiful.

Look for them at Fort Stevens State Park, Salishan Nature Trail, and Cape Blanco State Park. Uncommon year-round.

Quite vocal. Song is long and spirited and includes whistles, burrs, and call notes. Flight calls are a high "chip" or "whit."

Similar species: see House Finch entry page 243 and Purple Finch entry page 245.

Breeding male.
Changes from gray-brown nonbreeding plumage into bright yellow breeding plumage with a black forehead and wings. Bold wingbars.

Female/juvenile.
Female is drabber than male but gets yellower in breeding season. Bill changes from gray to pink for breeding in both sexes.

Male Lesser Goldfinch.
Darker overall with stubbier bill and yellower undertail coverts than American. Large white wing patch in flight.

Female Lesser Goldfinch.
Olive-gray with less white on the wings than the male.

AMERICAN GOLDFINCH

Spinus tristis

This bird's chipper call and bright colors make it a spring standout. Often detected by its flight call that sounds something like "po-ta-to chip!"

Found in open areas including weedy fields, streamside woodlands, farms, and neighborhoods. Diet is almost entirely seeds, especially those from thistles. Nest is a cup built in a shrub or tree. Forms large flocks in winter.

Look for them at Tillamook Bay Wetlands: Goodspeed Road, Nestucca Bay National Wildlife Refuge, and Cape Blanco State Park. Common May–October; rare to uncommon otherwise.

Song is a fast series of trills and burry phrases. Calls include a rising "zree" and short "dzik."

Lesser Goldfinch is rare except on the South Coast. Its call sounds sadder because it drops in pitch.

Male.
Distinctive dark hood and pale pink bill. Reddish brown back and pink or brown sides.

Female.
Paler than male, with gray hood and pinkish sides.

DARK-EYED JUNCO

Junco hyemalis (oreganus group)

This species varies in plumage across its range, and the most common type found at the coast is conveniently known as the Oregon Junco. The white-edged tail is helpfully present in all junco plumages.

Found in open areas with trees and bushes, including suburban areas. Eats seeds and arthropods found on the ground. Nest is a cup made of grass and lined with hair, usually placed on the ground where it is sheltered by low vegetation or logs. Sings from an elevated perch.

Look for them at Bayocean Peninsula, Brian Booth State Park, and Cape Blanco State Park. Very common in the winter and less common in the breeding season.

Song is a trill with even pitch and tempo. Calls include "tsipt" and a buzzy "dzit." Alarm call is a smacking chip.

Similar species: see Spotted Towhee entry page 263.

Adult.
Distinctive striped
head and a slight crest.
Bill is yellow-orange.

First winter.
Young birds are
dingier with brown
and gray stripes
on the head.

WHITE-CROWNED SPARROW

Zonotrichia leucophrys

This ubiquitous sparrow welcomes summer visitors to the coast with its enthusiastic song. Odds are good that a White-crowned Sparrow will be nearby whatever coastal parking lot you choose.

In the breeding season, prefers open areas with shrubs or small conifers and a mix of bare ground and grass. In winter, joins other sparrow species in weedy areas bordered by thick vegetation like blackberry hedges. Eats arthropods, seeds, and fruit, depending on the season. Sings from bushes and small trees.

Look for them at Nehalem Bay State Park, Mark Hatfield Marine Science Center and Estuary Trail, and Bullards Beach State Park. Very common April–July; common otherwise.

Sings loudly all day long in breeding season. Song begins with a whistle, then a fast series of notes, followed by a buzz. Calls include "sreet" and "pink."

Similar species: see Golden-crowned Sparrow entry page 255.

LENGTH: 7" / WINGSPAN: 9.5"

Adult breeding.
Large sparrow with
distinctive black
and yellow crown.

Adult nonbreeding.
Yellow and black crown markings are reduced. Young birds
have a little yellow on the front
of the crown but no black.

Adult White-throated Sparrow.
Crisply edged white throat and a thick
white or tan stripe above the eye.

GOLDEN-CROWNED SPARROW

Zonotrichia atricapilla

This winter visitor is often found in mixed flocks with other sparrow species. They continue to sing in fall, announcing their arrival with a mournful song.

 Found in weedy areas with brushy cover like blackberry bushes at the edges of fields or roadsides. Forages on the ground for seeds. Emerges slowly from shelter to feed, and retreats when disturbed.

Look for them at Cannon Beach Settling Ponds, Bayocean Peninsula, and Ni-Les'tun Overlook at Bandon Marsh National Wildlife Refuge. Common September–May.

Song is three long, descending whistles.
Call is a metallic "tseet" or "tew."

White-throated Sparrow is rare at the coast.
See also White-crowned Sparrow entry page 253.

Adult.
Breast is white with fine, brown streaks. Head is striped with yellow in front of eye. Prominent pale stripe down center of crown. Bill and legs are pink.

Nonbreeding adult Lapland Longspur.
Larger and plumper than sparrows, with a reddish wing patch and a buffy ear patch edged in black.

SAVANNAH SPARROW

Passerculus sandwichensis

Their buzzing and whirring insectlike songs can be heard coming from fence lines and fields of tall grass. Savannah Sparrows can be spotted hopping along open ground while foraging.

Found in open, grassy areas with patches of bare ground including fields, sewage ponds, and jetties. Eats invertebrates when available, supplementing with seeds and fruits. Nests on the ground, concealed by tall grass. Sings from fences and other perches.

Look for them at Fort Stevens State Park: South Jetty, Mark Hatfield Marine Science Center and Estuary Trail, and Rogue River South Jetty. Uncommon to common April–December; rare otherwise.

Song is a series of high, buzzy phrases. Calls include a high "tsew," and "tink" and "chip" alarm calls.

Lapland Longspur is rare in winter.

LENGTH: 5.5" / WINGSPAN: 8.75"

Adult.
Brown and gray stripes on the head. Brown streaks on a grayish breast concentrate in a central dark spot.

Adult Lincoln's Sparrow.
Fine, dark streaks on a buffy breast. The wide gray eyebrow also helps separate it from Song Sparrow.

SONG SPARROW

Melospiza melodia

These ubiquitous sparrows are often the first to pop up in response to pishing (squeaking and smacking sounds made by birders to coax birds into the open). Their barking alarm calls bring in more birds to investigate the threat.

Found in a variety of habitats that offer dense shrubs including neighborhoods, open forests, and edges of fields. Eats arthropods, seeds, and berries. Nests near the ground in a cup made from grass, protected by dense vegetation. Often perches conspicuously atop bushes when singing or calling.

Look for them at Cannon Beach Settling Ponds, Siletz Bay National Wildlife Refuge, and Lone Ranch State Wayside. Very common year-round.

Song begins with a couple repeated notes, followed by alternating buzzy and musical sections. Calls include "tseet," "tink," and a distinctive nasal "vimp."

Lincoln's Sparrow is uncommon September–April. Similar species: see also Fox Sparrow entry page 261.

LENGTH: 6.25" / WINGSPAN: 8.25"

Adult.
Large, chocolaty brown sparrow.
Breast heavily marked with brown
triangular spots. Bill is bicolored:
yellow below and darker on top.

FOX SPARROW

Passerella iliaca

The Oregon Coast is a winter home for the "Sooty" subspecies of this reticent sparrow. Fox Sparrows often call and forage under the cover of vegetation.

Found in forests with a thick understory of shrubs, in dense thickets, and in blackberry tangles. They uncover arthropods and seeds by hopping backward and raking their feet through the leaf litter.

Look for them at Nehalem Bay State Park, South Beach State Park, and Chetco Point Park. Common September–April.

Sings during migration. Song is a series of whistles and buzzes. Call is a loud "smack."

Similar species: see Song Sparrow entry page 259.

Male.
Large sparrow with red eyes and black upperparts. Corners of the tail are white. Both sexes have white spots and rufous sides.

Female.
Plumage dark brown where male's is black.

SPOTTED TOWHEE

Pipilo maculatus

Towhees are usually seen on the ground, scratching for food with their long claws. When rustling through dry leaves under bushes, they sound like a much larger animal.

Found in the brushy parts of open areas or forest edges. Feeds under shrubs like blackberry and salal. Eats seeds in winter and arthropods when available. Makes a cup nest on or near the ground, sheltered by plants.

Look for them at Kilchis Point Preserve, South Beach State Park, and Bullards Beach State Park. Common year-round.

Song is a trill that sounds like "turweee." Calls include a high "tink," a buzzy "tseereet," and a burry wheeze.

Similar species: see Dark-eyed Junco entry page 251.

Male.
Thick, pointed bill. Red shoulder patch with a yellow stripe below.

Female.
Streaky brown with a striped face and rufous tones on the wings.

RED-WINGED BLACKBIRD

Agelaius phoeniceus

This descriptively named bird is almost always heard on wetland birding trips. The showy males can cover their red wing patches or flare them out, depending on the signal they want to send.

Found in wetlands with cattails or tall grasses, where males display and sing conspicuously. Attacks larger birds and drives them away from its territory. Diet includes seeds, grain, and insects. Nest is a woven cup of grasses in wetland vegetation.

Look for them at Sitka Sedge State Natural Area, Beaver Creek State Natural Area, and Bandon Marsh National Wildlife Refuge. Common year-round.

Vocalize frequently. Male song is "Kong-ka-REE-ga" (mnemonic: "Pumpkin EAT-er.") Female song is a high rattle or a harsh "cheer." Calls include "chunk" and "jenk."

Female Red-winged Blackbirds are often mistaken for sparrows but note their pointed bills and longer legs.

Male.
Small blackbird with a thick bill. Glossy black with a distinctive brown head.

Female.
Brown with a pale throat.

Juvenile.
Streaky brown with a scaled pattern on the back.

BROWN-HEADED COWBIRD

Molothrus ater

Cowbirds are brood parasites, laying eggs in the nests of other birds instead of building their own. Host birds include sparrows, warblers, flycatchers, and blackbirds. Young cowbirds find each other and form small flocks after they leave their foster parents.

Found in fields, coastal scrub, pastures, and along woodland edges. Diet varies seasonally, including insects and weed seeds. In winter, they join flocks of other blackbirds at spilled grain piles. Small groups of males gather around a female to sing and display in the spring.

Look for them at Wireless Road near Astoria, Mark Hatfield Marine Science Center and Estuary Trail, and Arizona Beach State Recreation Site. Common April–July and uncommon outside of the breeding season.

Song is a series of rising gurgles and whistles. Both sexes give a chattery rattle call.

Similar species: see Brewer's Blackbird entry page 269.

Male.
Long tail, thin
bill, and pale eyes.
Plumage is black
with glossy tones
of violet and green.

Female.
Brown with some iridescence
on the wings. Eyes are dark.

BREWER'S BLACKBIRD

Euphagus cyanocephalus

These brash birds are easy to get a close view of, but the beauty of their lustrous plumage is underappreciated, perhaps because they are often seen eating dropped food in parking lots.

Found in pastures, wetlands, and parking lots, and along roadsides. Eats insects and plant matter obtained by flycatching or walking on the ground. Also feeds on spilled grain at dairy farms, especially in the nonbreeding season. Nests in bushes or wetland vegetation.

Look for them in grocery store parking lots, at D River Beach Wayside, along roads around Tillamook, and at Coquille River South Jetty. Common year-round.

Songs include a high "creak" and a warbling "gurgle." Gives a variety of calls including "churr," "chatter," "chuk," and many musical sounds.

See Brown-headed Cowbird entry page 267.

Adult.
Drab olive-yellow
warbler with a very
inconspicuous orange
crown. Darker line
through the eye.

**Female
Yellow Warbler.**
Plain face lacking the
Orange-crowned's dark
line through its eye.

ORANGE-CROWNED WARBLER

Leiothlypis celata

Not exactly the colorful spectacle their name implies, but a welcome harbinger of spring. A few hardy individuals over-winter along the coast, usually in brushy areas near water.

 Often found in shrubs and small trees. Feeds on small invertebrates plucked from leaves. Nests on the ground below vegetation near streams. Also uses shrubby areas in clear-cuts.

Look for them at Yaquina Head Outstanding Natural Area, Devil's Elbow State Park, and Bullards Beach State Park. Common April–July and rare in winter.

Song is an unsteady trill that is lower in pitch and often slower at the end. Call is a metallic "chip."

Female Yellow Warbler is uncommon May–September.

Male.
Yellow throat and distinctive black mask, bordered by white above.

Female.
Lacks the mask but has a yellow throat and undertail.

COMMON YELLOWTHROAT

Geothlypis trichas

Dashing but secretive, this widespread warbler allows only occasional glimpses. Males often sing from cover, but lucky or determined birders may spot their telltale mask.

Known for skulking in cattails and tall grass, yellow-throats take some patience to see but may pop up to investigate the "pishing" or squeaky noises birders make. Feeds on invertebrates in marshes as well as fields with tall grass or shrubs like Nootka rose along the edge. Makes a cup nest on or near the ground.

Look for them at Astoria Mitigation Bank Wetlands, Sitka Sedge State Natural Area, and Bandon Marsh National Wildlife Refuge. Yellowthroats arrive earlier and stay later than many warblers. Common April–September.

One of the easiest warbler songs to identify and remember. A series of whistled phrases that sounds like "wichity-wichity-wichity." Call is a low, resonant "chup" or "churt."

Black mask is unique.

Breeding male "Audubon's." Yellow cap and chin, yellow throat.

Breeding male "Myrtle." Black mask, white throat.

Female "Audubon's." Yellow throat but no cap. Drabber than male.

Female "Myrtle." Drabber than male, with a dark ear patch and a whitish throat.

YELLOW-RUMPED WARBLER

Setophaga coronata

Both the "Myrtle" and "Audubon's" subspecies of this ostentatious warbler can be found along the coast. Though the plumage varies among subspecies and sexes, the yellow sides and rump are constants.

Found in a broad range of habitats during the winter. "Myrtles" can appropriately be found foraging in myrtles and other native coastal vegetation. Eats arthropods and sometimes berries. Easy to spot fluttering from branch to branch in low trees and bushes in pursuit of invertebrates.

Look for both subspecies in winter at Chetco Point Park, Brian Booth State Park, and Fort Stevens State Park. Common October–April and uncommon in summer. "Myrtle" found at the coast only during the winter and nests in the boreal forest. "Audubon's" stays longer and moves up in altitude to breed.

Song typically consists of simple, repeated, warbling couplets. Call is a low "chwit."

Similar species: see Townsend's Warbler entry page 277.

LENGTH: 5.5" / WINGSPAN: 9.25"

Male.
Black cap, mask, and
throat. Yellow breast,
black streaks on the sides.

Female.
Similar in pattern to male
but more olive green in color.

**Male Black-throated
Gray Warbler.**
Contrasting stripes on the
face, a black throat, and
black streaks on a white belly.

TOWNSEND'S WARBLER

Setophaga townsendi

A bright treat in the winter when most other warblers have left for warmer climes. Sometimes joins mixed foraging flocks in winter with chickadees, kinglets, and nuthatches.

In winter, found in spruce, alder, and Douglas-fir trees. Also found in parks and yards where it may visit suet feeders. Nests in conifers in mountain forests. Feeds on invertebrates in the foliage of trees and can be found by listening for its chip notes.

Look for them at Ecola State Park, Cape Perpetua, and Harris Beach State Park. Uncommon to common September–May.

Song is a buzzy series of phrases, often rising. More slurred than the similar songs of Hermit and Black-throated Gray Warblers. Call is a sharp "chip."

Black-throated Gray Warbler is uncommon to common April–September. Similar species: see also Hermit Warbler entry page 279.

Male.
Yellow face and black throat. Prominent white wing bars.

Female.
Face is dingy yellow. Lacks a black throat.

HERMIT WARBLER

Setophaga occidentalis

This appropriately named warbler is more easily heard than seen, often hidden in the tree canopy. It sounds similar to Townsend's Warbler and Black-throated Gray Warbler, but habitat and seasonality help to distinguish between them.

Prefers stands of tall Douglas-firs but is also found in coastal spruces. Feeds on small invertebrates high in the canopy and often sings from the treetops. Makes a small cup nest in a conifer.

Look for them at Cape Perpetua, Nestucca Bay National Wildlife Refuge, and Cape Meares State Park. Common May–July.

Song is a series of buzzy phrases, often with a higher last note. Variable and similar to songs of Townsend's Warbler and Black-throated Gray Warbler. Call is a sharp "chip."

Hybridizes with Townsend's Warblers (page 277). Hybrids often have a clean yellow face and a black throat, with a yellow chest.

LENGTH: 5" / WINGSPAN: 8"

Male.
Yellow face and breast and an olive back. Distinctive black cap is reduced in females.

Male Yellow Warbler.
Yellow edges on wing feathers, reddish streaks on breast, and no cap.

WILSON'S WARBLER

Cardellina pusilla

This bright and noisy warbler hangs out near eye level, making it easy to enjoy. Wilson's Warblers look like bouncing yellow balls as they hover and flycatch to grab insects from leaves and twigs.

Prefers forested areas with understory shrubs. Nests on the ground or low in vegetation like ferns or blackberry vines. Eats invertebrates including spiders, aphids, and moth and butterfly larvae.

Look for them at Cape Lookout State Park, South Slough National Estuarine Research Reserve, and Harris Beach State Park. Very common April–July and less common August–September.

Sings frequently and loudly. Song is a series of sharp notes that speeds up, like a car engine that won't start. Call is a sharp "jit."

Yellow Warbler is uncommon May–September.

Breeding male.
Unmistakable with a vivid reddish orange head, bright yellow body, and black wings.

Female.
Females are drabber olive-yellow with grayish wings. Both sexes have bold wingbars and thick bills.

WESTERN TANAGER

Piranga ludoviciana

These eye-popping birds decorate trees like ornaments when they arrive in spring. Shade-grown coffee farms provide winter habitat in Central America for tanagers, where deforestation has caused habitat loss.

During the breeding season, prefers conifer or mixed forests with some openings, but is more generalist in migration. Often sings or calls from high in a tree. Feeds on insects including wasps and beetles, and also eats berries and other fruits.

Look for them at Knight County Park, Beaver Creek State Natural Area, and Millicoma Marsh. Uncommon to common May–September. Most conspicuous during migration in May.

Song is a series of short phrases that is burrier and slower than an American Robin's song. Call is a dry "chippit" that sometimes sound like "chippitee" or "chippituk."

Female resembles a large warbler with a thicker bill.

Breeding male.
Chunky bird with a
hefty bill. Black head
and bright orange belly.

Female.
Females and juve-
niles have pale stripes on
their heads and streaked
buffy or orange bellies

Male Evening Grosbeak.
Large, pale green bill, bold
yellow eyebrow, and large
white wing patches.

BLACK-HEADED GROSBEAK

Pheucticus melanocephalus

Loud in both voice and color, these birds fill the air with exuberant song. Males also perform eye-catching display flights, singing while fluttering their black and white wings and tails.

Found in mixed conifer and deciduous forests near streams. Nests primarily in deciduous trees. Consumes both insects and berries. Both males and females sing, and do so while sitting on the nest.

Look for them at Beaver Creek State Natural Area, Nestucca Bay National Wildlife Refuge, and Bandon Marsh National Wildlife Refuge. Common May–August.

Sings loudly and frequently. Song is a series of musical phrases, sung quickly. Sounds sweeter and faster than American Robin. Call is a short "wink" or "kwik."

Evening Grosbeak is rare to uncommon April–October.

ACCESSIBLE BIRDING SITES ON THE OREGON COAST

Presented from north to south. Please research whether these sites meet your particular needs before visiting.

Kilchis Point Preserve
A flat, paved trail leads to views of Tillamook Bay.

Cape Meares State Park
Two overlooks near the parking lot provide ocean views.

Nestucca Bay National Wildlife Refuge
An overlook provides views of fields where geese winter. A paved trail goes uphill through restored prairie to another overlook.

Depoe Bay Whale Watching Center
Views of whales as well as rocky shore and ocean birds.

Yaquina Head Outstanding Natural Area
Offers a visitor center, overlooks of seabird nesting areas, and an accessible tidepool area.

Bandon Marsh National Wildlife Refuge
An overlook with a view of estuary mudflats.

Coquille Point
A viewpoint that looks out over offshore rocks with nesting seabirds.

Harris Beach State Park
Offers an ADA accessible ramp to the beach and viewpoints for watching birds on Goat Island.

RECOMMENDED RESOURCES

Site Guides
Birding Oregon: A Guide to the Best Birding Sites Across the State by John Rakestraw
Oregon Coast Birding Trail oregoncoastbirding.com

Oregon Coast Audubon Chapters
Audubon Society of Lincoln City lincolncityaudubon.org
Cape Arago Audubon capearagoaudubon.org
Kalmiopsis Audubon Society kalmiopsisaudubon.org

Pelagic Birding Tours
Oregon Pelagic Tours oregonpelagictours.com

Birding by Ear
Peterson Field Guide to Bird Sounds of Western North America by Nathan Pieplow

Comprehensive Field Guides
National Geographic Field Guide to the Birds of North America by Jonathan Alderfer and Jon L. Dunn
The Sibley Guide to Birds by David Sibley

Birding and Conservation Organizations
American Bird Conservancy abcbirds.org
American Birding Association aba.org
National Audubon Society audubon.org
Oregon Birding Association oregonbirding.org
Portland Audubon portlandaudubon.org

ACKNOWLEDGMENTS

I signed the contract for this book in February 2020, not anticipating the massive changes that would soon come to birding, travel, and daily life. My family has been a constant source of support and sometimes baked goods. Thank you to Max, Greta, Alan, Owen, Mom, and Dad. My dog, Rosie, has also been excellent company through these long months. Thank you to the friends that cheered me on, read my drafts, and celebrated Owloween with me over Zoom. I missed going birding, drinking beer, and having potlucks with you all. I also want to thank my mental healthcare providers for helping me get through a hard year. No one should feel ashamed to reach out for help when they need it.

Though many of my own observations are included in this book, the base of knowledge that I drew from for much of it came from ornithologists and birders that came before me. In particular, the late Dave Marshall and the other editors and contributors that worked together to create *Birds of Oregon, A General Reference*, an outstanding compendium of information on the state's birds. Thank you also to Nathan Pieplow for generously allowing me to borrow his insightful descriptions of bird sounds from his pioneering book *Peterson Field Guide to Bird Sounds of Western North America*.

Thank you to Portland Audubon for standing up for Oregon's birds for over 100 years. Many of the birds in this book have benefited from the tireless conservation work of its staff and volunteers.

Will McKay and the talented staff at Timber Press are a pleasure to work with, and they make beautiful books. Thank you for giving me the chance to write this love letter to the Oregon Coast's birds and unique places. Thank you also to the photographers whose work brings the birds in this book to life. Your skill, patience, and artistic eye are awe inspiring. This book wouldn't exist without your contributions.

To everyone who kept asking me when I was going to write another book: here it is! Thank you for reminding me to think of myself as a writer.

PHOTO AND ILLUSTRATION CREDITS

NAGI ABOULENEIN, page 158 upper middle

AUDREY ADDISON, pages 42 bottom, 72 top, 84 bottom, 132 middle, 158 bottom, 172 bottom, 188, 200 middle, 206 top, 216 bottom, 220 bottom, 244 top, 248 top, 256 bottom, 260, 274 top, 276 middle and bottom, 280 bottom, 284 bottom

A nature lover at heart, Audrey's passion for birding blossomed in the Pacific Northwest. She can be found on Instagram @tweetsandchirps.

ANGELA CALABRESE, pages 12, 104 bottom, 114 top, 134 lower middle, 146 top, 198 top, 204 top and bottom, 240 bottom, 246 top, 264 top, 266 top, 274 bottom

Angela is a PNW native and began photographing birds as a teenager. See more of Angela's photography on Instagram @angela.calabrese.photography.

ERIC CARLSON, pages 2, 9, 48, 56 top, 60 middle, 76 top, 82 top, 96 bottom, 108 top and middle, 110 top and middle, 112 bottom, 118 bottom, 120 top, 122 bottom, 126 middle, 128 bottom, 136 bottom, 148 bottom, 150 bottom, 154 top, 156 top, 158 top, 160, 162 middle, 168, 170 upper middle, 178 bottom, 184 bottom, 190 bottom, 192, 196 bottom, 198 bottom, 204 middle, 208, 212, 214, 226, 228 top, 234 top, 236 bottom, 240 top, 242 top, 248 bottom, 250 top, 252 bottom, 254 top and bottom, 258, 262 bottom, 268 bottom, 272 top, 274 middle two, 280 top, 282 top

Eric is a Portland-based bird admirer, photographer, and author of *Neighborhood Birding 101*. Find more of his photos on Instagram @portlandbirder.

KEN CHAMBERLAIN, page 152 bottom

EMILIE CHEN, pages 50 top, 54 bottom, 58 bottom, 60 top and bottom, 62 top and bottom, 64 top, 70 top, 78 bottom, 90 top, 92 bottom, 96 top, 100 middle, 104 upper middle, 116 bottom, 130 middle, 132 top, 134 bottom, 138, 144 bottom, 146 bottom, 164 bottom, 166 bottom, 170 lower middle, 174 upper middle, 176 bottom, 178 middle, 182 middle, 186 top, 190 top, 200 bottom, 202 lower middle, 210, 222, 224 top, 228 bottom, 232, 234 bottom, 248 lower middle, 250 bottom, 252 top, 254 middle, 262 top, 268 top, 270, 272 bottom, 276 top, 282 bottom

Emilie began birding and photographing birds in Southern California in 2013. She now lives in Portland, Oregon, and posts new work to Instagram @watchingtrees.

DON HENISE, page 162 top

MARK LEE, page 206 bottom

MAUREEN LEONG-KEE, page 82 bottom

ROBERT LOCKETT, pages 158 lower middle, 202 upper middle

BRETT LOVELACE AND OREGON STATE UNIVERSITY, page 18

Brett is a biologist studying Marbled Murrelets.

ROY W. LOWE, pages 19, 20, 21, 36 top and middle, 38, 40 top, 42 top, 44 top, 46, 50 bottom, 52 top, 54 top and middle, 56 bottom, 58 top, 62 middle, 64 bottom, 66, 68, 70 bottom, 72 middle and bottom row, 74, 76 middle two, 78 top, 80, 84 top, 86, 88, 90 bottom, 92 top and middle, 94, 98 top, 100 top and bottom, 102, 104 top and lower middle, 106, 110 bottom, 112 top, 116 top, 118 top, 122 middle, 126 top and bottom, 128 top, 130 top and bottom, 132 middle and bottom row, 134 upper middle, 136 top, 140, 142, 144 top, 148 top, 150 top, 152 top, 154 bottom, 156 bottom, 162 bottom, 164 top, 166 top, 170 top, 172 top, 174 top and lower middle, 176 except bottom, 180, 182 bottom, 194, 196 top, 200 top, 220 top, 230, 236 top, 238, 264 bottom, 266 middle and bottom, 284 top and middle

Roy is a former national wildlife refuge manager and spends much of his time in retirement observing and photographing wildlife. Find his photos on Instagram @ rloweiii.

NICHOLAS MARTENS, pages 98 bottom, 248 upper middle

KAYLA MCCURRY, pages 36 bottom, 40 middle, 76 bottom, 136 middle, 170 bottom, 174 bottom, 242 bottom, 246 middle

Kayla is a lifelong Oregonian who loves watching birds and capturing their lives on camera. Find her on Instagram @shes-abirder.

GERRY MEENAGHAN, page 134 top

ERIC PRATT, page 40 bottom

JON PUGMIRE, pages 44 bottom, 98 middle, 114 bottom, 278 top

W. DOUGLAS ROBINSON, page 278 bottom

JEN SANFORD, pages 52 bottom, 108 bottom, 120 bottom, 122 top, 178 top, 182 top, 184 top, 186 bottom, 202 top, 216 top, 218, 224 bottom, 244 bottom, 246 bottom, 256 top

Jen enjoys five-mile-radius birding in Vancouver, Washington; and Lincoln City, Oregon. Find her photos on Instagram @ iusedtohatebirds.

JACK WILLIAMSON, page 202 bottom

Alcids silhouette on pages 24 and 37–45 based on a photo by DickDaniels (http://carolinabirds.org) / Wikimedia Commons (used under a CCA-SA 3.0 Unported license)

Geese & Ducks silhouette on pages 25 and 47–81 by Kristtaps/iStock.com

Coots silhouette on pages 25 and 83 and Vultures silhouette on pages 6, 29, and 167 by iDrawSilhouettes/creativefabrica.com

Loons silhouette on pages 6, 25, and 85–89 by Rahul Kolgaonkar/pngitem.com

Grebes silhouette on pages 26 and 91–97, Plovers silhouette on pages 27 and 109–

115, Sandpipers silhouette on pages 27 and 117–143, and Gulls & Terns silhouette on pages 28 and 151–165, and Kingfishers silhouette on page 30 and 185, and Blackbirds silhouette on pages 35 and 265–269 by Birchside/gograph.com

Cormorants silhouette on pages 6, 26, and 99–103 by piranjya/iStock.com

Pelicans silhouette on pages 6, 26, and 105 from pngitem.com

Oystercatchers silhouette on pages 6, 27, and 107 by ilyasov/iStock.com

Herons & Egrets silhouette on pages 6, 28, and 145–147 by rangepuppies/iStock.com

Shearwaters silhouette on pages 28 and 149 based on a photo by hstiver/iStock.com

Osprey, Hawks & Eagles silhouette on pages 29 and 169–177 by vadimmmus/iStock.com

Hawk silhouette on page 4 and Falcons silhouette on pages 29 and 179–181 by PetrP/shutterstock.com

Pigeons & Doves silhouette on page 30 and 183 by DeCe_X/iStock.com

Woodpeckers silhouette on page 30 and 187–191 from pinclipart.com

Jays, Crows & Ravens silhouette on page 6, 31, and 193–197 by Vector SpMan/shutterstock.com

Hummingbirds silhouette on pages 6, 31, and 199–201 by mr.Timmi/shutterstock.com

Swallows silhouette on pages 6, 31, and 203–211 by Ivana Kontic/shutterstock.com

Chickadees silhouette on pages 32 and 213–215 and Wrentit silhouette on pages 32 and 217 from SilhouetteGarden.com

Kinglets silhouette on pages 32 and 219 based on an illustration by Viktoria Karpunina/shutterstock.com

Flycatchers silhouette on pages 33 and 225–227 by Natasha Sinegina / creazilla.com (used under a CCA 4.0 license)

Wrens silhouette on pages 33 and 229–233 by Loveleen/stock.adobe.com

Thrushes silhouette on pages 33 and 235–239 by Jackie/cleanpng.com

Waxwings silhouette on pages 34 and 241 by Bob Comix / creazilla.com (used under a CCA 4.0 license)

Finches silhouette on pages 6, 34, and 243–249 by Stefanie Schubbert / shutterstock.com

Sparrows silhouette on pages 34 and 251–263 by Noah Strycker / shutterstock.com

Warblers silhouette on pages 35 and 271–281 by thesilhouettequeen/123rf.com

Tanagers & Grosbeaks silhouette on pages 35 and 283–285 based on an illustration by AlsuSh/shutterstock.com

BIBLIOGRAPHY

Betts, M. G., Northrup, J. M., Guerrero, J. A. B., et al. 2020. Squeezed by a habitat split: Warm ocean conditions and old-forest loss interact to reduce long-term occupancy of a threatened seabird. *Conservation Letters* 13: e12745.

Billerman, S. M., B. K. Keeney, P. G. Rodewald, and T. S. Schulenberg, eds. 2020. Birds of the World (website). Ithaca, New York: Cornell Laboratory of Ornithology. birdsoftheworld.org/bow/home.

Cornell Lab of Ornithology. 2020. All About Birds (website). Ithaca, New York: Cornell Lab of Ornithology. allaboutbirds.org.

Dunne, P., and K. T. Karlson. 2019. *Gulls Simplified*. Princeton, New Jersey: Princeton University Press.

eBird. 2021. eBird: An online database of bird distribution and abundance (website). eBird, Cornell Lab of Ornithology, Ithaca, New York. ebird.org.

Gaines, E. P. 2019. Western Snowy Plovers: A conservation success story for Oregon. *Oregon Birds* 45(1): 28.

Howell, S. N. G., and J. L. Dunn. 2007. *A Reference Guide to Gulls of the Americas*. Peterson Reference Guide Series. Boston: Houghton Mifflin.

Imperiled Species: Marbled Murrelet. (n.d.) Retrieved from: *https://audubonportland.org/our-work/protect/habitat-and-wildlife/imperiled-species/marbled-murrelet/*

Important Bird Areas: East Sand Island. (n.d.) Retrieved from: *www.audubon.org/important-bird-areas/east-sand-island*

Kaufman, K. 2011. *Kaufman Field Guide to Advanced Birding: Understanding What You See and Hear*. New York: Houghton Mifflin Harcourt.

Liebezeit, J. et al. 2020. Black oystercatcher (*Haematopus bachmani*) population size, use of marine reserve complexes, and spatial distribution in Oregon. *Northwestern Naturalist* 101, no. 1: 14.

Marshall, D. B., Hunter, M. G., Contreras, A. 2003. *Birds of Oregon: A General Reference*. Corvallis, Oregon: Oregon State University Press.

Meet Goose #579, One of a Distinguished Few. (n.d.) Retrieved from: *www.fws.gov/nwrs/threecolumn.aspx?id=2147584988*

Myers, B. M. et al. 2019. Behavioral and morphological evidence of an Allen's × Rufous hummingbird (*Selasphorus sasin* × *S. rufus*) hybrid zone in southern Oregon and northern California. *The Auk*, 136(4).

Nelson, K. and P. Engelmeyer. 2020. Marbled Murrelet ecology and conservation presentation for Portland Audubon delivered on July 16, 2020.

Pieplow, N. 2019. *Field Guide to the Bird Sounds of Western North America*. New York: Houghton Mifflin Harcourt.

Shewey, J., and T. Blount. 2017. *Birds of the Pacific Northwest*. Ed. Hendrik Herlyn. Portland, Oregon: Timber Press.

Sibley, D. 2014. *The Sibley Guide to Birds*. 2nd ed. New York: Alfred A. Knopf. 2014.

Stephenson, T., and S. Whittle. 2013. *The Warbler Guide*. Princeton, New Jersey: Princeton University Press.

Swanson, S., and M. Smith. 2013. *Must-see Birds of the Pacific Northwest*. 1st ed. Portland, Oregon: Timber Press.

INDEX

A

abundance, defined, 23

abundance by month
April–August, 203, 211, 229
April–December, 257
April–July, 245, 253, 267, 271, 281
April–May, 117, 119, 133, 135, 137, 141
April–October, 285
April–September, 45, 165, 203, 209, 223, 225, 273, 277
August–April, 91
August–May, 55, 95
August–October, 155
August–September, 133, 149, 165, 237, 281
February–September, 201
July–April, 123, 125
July–May, 143
July–November, 157
July–October, 119, 137
July–September, 133, 135, 141
June–August, 89
June–November, 151
March–August, 39
March–October, 169, 183
March–September, 117, 167, 205, 207
May–August, 285
May–July, 225, 237, 279
May–October, 241, 249
May–September, 99, 271, 281, 283
November–April, 75, 77, 163
November–February, 179
November–January, 41
October–April, 61, 65, 79, 97, 275
October–December, 159
October–May, 47, 59, 67, 81
September–April, 53, 73, 83, 153, 159, 261
September–May, 125, 221, 255, 277

accessibility
accessible birding sites on the Oregon Coast, 286
beaches offering wheelchairs, 19
driving on the beach, 12–13
Oregon State Parks accessible features, 19

Accipitridae family, 29
Actitis macularius, 139
Aechmophorus occidentalis, 97
Agelaius phoeniceus, 265
albatrosses, 13
Alcedinidae family, 30
Alcidae family, 24
alcids, 13, 24, 36–45
Allen's Hummingbird, 200, 201
American Birding Association (ABA), 20
American Coot, 82–83
American Crow, 194–195
American Golden-Plover, 109
American Goldfinch, 248–249

American Kestrel, 178–179
American Ornithological Society, 21
American Robin, 238–239
American White Pelican, 104, 105
American Wigeon, 60–61
amphipods, 12
Anas acuta, 63
Anas crecca, 53
Anas platyrhynchos, 59
Anatidae family, 25
Ancient Murrelet, 41
Anna's Hummingbird, 198–199
Ardea alba, 147
Ardea herodias, 145
Ardeidae family, 28
Ardenna grisea, 149
Arenaria melanocephala, 121
Aythya collaris, 65
Aythya marila, 67

B

Baird's Sandpiper, 132, 133
Bald Eagle, 176–177
bald heads as adaptation, 29
Band-tailed pigeon, 182–183
Bank Swallow, 204, 205
Barn Swallow, 208–209
Barrow's Goldeneye, 76, 77
bays and estuaries as habitat, 10–11
Belted Kingfisher, 184–185
Bewick's Wren, 232–233
bills, shapes and functions.
  See specific bird family descriptions, 24–35
binoculars and scopes, 18
birding community, inclusivity, 21

birding sites
  Alder Creek Farm in Manzanita, 201
  Alsea Bay Boat Docks, 75
  Arizona Beach State Recreation Site, 183, 187, 211, 241, 267
  Astoria Mitigation Bank Wetlands, 57, 205, 231, 273
  Bandon Marsh National Wildlife Refuge, 11, 15, 49, 53, 57, 75, 113, 119, 129, 133, 135, 143, 171, 173, 175, 205, 231, 265, 273, 285
  Bandon State Natural Area, 117
  Barview Jetty, 43, 85, 95, 123, 141
  Bayocean Peninsula, 11, 47, 61, 63, 67, 81, 83, 129, 133, 165, 217, 251, 255
  Beaver Creek State Natural Area, 187, 191, 205, 245, 265, 283, 285
  Boiler Bay State Scenic Viewpoint, 13, 101, 107, 149
  Boiler Bay State Wayside, 87
  Brian Booth State Park, 113, 139, 153, 157, 223, 251, 275
  Bullards Beach State Park, 127, 165, 191, 221, 253, 263, 271
  Cannon Beach Settling Ponds, 15, 91, 139, 187, 213, 223, 227, 255, 259

Cape Arago State Park, 11, 41, 43, 69, 85, 101, 105, 149, 167, 177
Cape Blanco State Park, 97, 179, 219, 247, 249, 251
Cape Lookout State Park, 281
Cape Meares Lake, 79
Cape Meares State Park, 71, 101, 181, 215, 219, 279
Cape Perpetua, 14, 41, 193, 197, 207, 225, 235, 277, 279
Charleston Boat Basin, 47, 51, 67, 95
Chetco Point Park, 13, 41, 73, 89, 139, 153, 209, 227, 261, 275
Circle Creek Conservation Area, 241
Clay Myers State Natural Area, 221
Coos Bay North Spit: Weyco Settling Pond, 137
Coquille Point, 37
Coquille River jetties, 107, 141, 169
Coquille River South Jetty, 121, 131, 269
Crissey Field State Park, 159, 173, 223
Dean Creek Elk Viewing Area, 211
Del Rey Beach, 109, 117
Devil's Elbow State Park, 271
D River Beach Wayside, 159, 269

East Devil's Lake State Recreation Area, 79, 91
Eckman Lake, 57, 65, 143
Ecola State Park, 14, 73, 207, 219, 225, 229, 277
Face Rock Wayside, 45, 161
Fort Clatsop National Memorial on the Netul River Trail, 67
Fort Stevens State Park, 12, 87, 103, 135, 165, 171, 191, 193, 247, 275
Fort Stevens State Park: South Jetty, 87, 105, 149, 151, 257
Fort Stevens State Park: Parking Area D, 113, 119, 129
Garibaldi Marina, 77
Gold Beach harbor, 59, 155
Gold Beach marina, 79
Goodspeed Road, Beaver Creek State Natural Area, 175
Goodspeed Road, Nestucca Bay National Wildlife Refuge, 249
Goodspeed Road, Yaquina Bay South Jetty, 155
Harris Beach State Park, 39, 45, 99, 189, 197, 199, 217, 237, 277, 281
Haystack Rock near Cannon Beach, 11, 39, 45, 69, 99, 107, 161
Haystack Rock near Pacific City, 105
Honeyman State Park, 235

birding sites (*cont.*)

Humbug Mountain State Park, 14, 193, 207, 215, 229

Kilchis Point Preserve, 263

Knight County Park, 169, 283

Lake Lytle, 65

Lone Ranch State Wayside, 245, 259

Mark Hatfield Marine Science Center and Estuary Trail, 11, 47, 61, 103, 109, 119, 135, 169, 171, 203, 253, 257, 267

Mike Miller County Park, 215, 221, 229

Millicoma Marsh, 15, 55, 61, 63, 77, 83, 213, 227, 243, 283

Necanicum Estuary National History Park, 59

Necanicum River Estuary, 185

Nehalem Bay State Park, 12, 89, 111, 157, 245, 253, 261

Nehalem Sewage Ponds, 137

Neskowin Beach Golf Course, 53

Nestucca Bay National Wildlife Refuge, 14, 49, 51, 59, 167, 177, 179, 183, 189, 201, 237, 279, 285

Netarts Bay, 75, 93, 147

Netarts Bay Boat Basin, 203

Ni-Les'tun Overlook at Bandon Marsh National Wildlife Refuge, 255

Oregon Dunes Recreation Area, 12

Oswald West State Park, 189, 197, 235

Port of Brookings Harbor, 93, 103

Port Orford, 87

Port Orford Heads State Park, 71

Rogue River South Jetty, 121, 157, 257

Salishan Nature Trail, 55, 77, 109, 131, 137, 199, 213, 241, 247

Salmon Harbor Marina, 93, 203

Seal Rock State Park, 123

Seaside Cove, 13, 85, 97, 121

Siletz Bay National Wildlife Refuge, 63, 259

Siltcoos River mouth, 111

Siltcoos River: Waxmyrtle Trail, 183, 185, 201, 217

Sitka Sedge State Natural Area, 111, 127, 131, 143, 185, 231, 265, 273

Siuslaw River North Jetty, 159

Siuslaw River South Jetty, 81, 209

South Beach State Park, 117, 261, 263

South Slough National Estuarine Research Reserve, 11, 225, 237, 281

Strawberry Hill Wayside, 71

Sunset Beach Recreation Area, 127, 209, 243

Three Arch Rocks National Wildlife Refuge viewed from Oceanside, 37

Tillamook, along roads, 269

Tillamook, fields and pastures around, 163, 173, 179

Tillamook Bay and farm fields to the east, 147

Tillamook Bay Wetlands, 155, 175, 249

Tillamook River Wetlands, 14, 15

Umpqua River South, 73

Umpqua River South Jetty, 133, 151

Warrenton Waterfront Trail, 55

Westlake County Park, 65

Wireless Road near Astoria, 14, 49, 153, 211, 267

Yachats Commons Park, 199

Yachats State Park, 121, 141

Yaquina Bay, 39, 53, 147

Yaquina Bay South Jetty, 89, 95, 151

Yaquina Bay State Park, 243

Yaquina Head Outstanding Natural Area, 11, 37, 43, 69, 97, 99, 161, 167, 177, 181, 271

Young's Bay, 83

birding tips
  cautions when exploring
    mudflats, 11
  at high and low tide, 11–12
  listening for bird sounds,
    14, 15
  viewing canopy-dwelling
    birds, 14
  viewing ocean birds, 13
#BirdNamesForBirds
  campaign, 21
birds named after people,
  21
birds of prey, adaptations,
  29
bird sounds
  forests, 14
  freshwater wetlands, 15
  "pishing", 34
  songs and calls, 23, 35
Black-bellied Plover, 11,
  108–109
blackbirds, 35, 264–269
Black-capped Chickadee,
  212–213
Black-headed Grosbeak,
  284–285
Black Oystercatcher, 8, 11,
  12, 16, 106–107
Black Phoebe, 14. 33,
  226–227
Black Scoter, 71, 72, 73
Black-throated Gray
  Warbler, 276, 277, 279
Black Turnstone, 8, 11,
  120–121, 123
Bombycilla cedrorum, 241
Bombycillidae family, 34
*Brachyramphus marmora-
  tus*, 41

Brandt's Cormorant, 8,
  98–99
Brant, 11, 46–47
Branta bernicla, 47
Branta canadensis, 51
Branta hutchinsii, 49
Brewer's Blackbird,
  268–269
Brown-headed Cowbird,
  266–267
Brown Pelican, 8, 16,
  104–105, 151
Bucephala albeola, 75
Bucephala clangula, 77
Bufflehead, 74–75
Bushtit, 216, 217
Buteo jamaicensis, 175
Buteo lineatus, 173

C

Cackling Goose, 48–49
Calidris alba, 126
Calidris alpina, 129
Calidris mauri, 133
Calidris minutilla, 131
Calidris virgata, 123
California Gull, 153, 156–157
California Scrub-Jay, 192,
  193
Calypte anna, 199
Canada Goose, 50–51
  Dusky subspecies, 50, 51
carbon emissions, 17
Cardellina pusilla, 281
Cardinalidae family, 35
Caspian Tern, 11, 164–165
Cathartes aura, 167
Cathartidae family, 29
Catharus ustulatus, 237
Cedar Waxwing, 34,
  240–241

Cephhus columba, 39
Cerorhinca monocerata, 43
Chamaea fasciata, 217
Charadriidae family, 27
Charadrius nivosus nivosus,
  111
Charadrius semipalmatus,
  113
Charadrius vociferus, 116
Chestnut-backed Chickadee,
  214–215, 219
chickadees
  bird sounds, 32
  in mixed-species flocks,
    14, 187, 221, 277
  species profiles, 212–215
Cinnamon Teal, 52
Circus hudsonius, 171
Cistothorus palustris, 231
Clark's Grebe, 96, 97
Cliff Swallow, 210–211
climate change, 16
coastal birds
  habitat destruction, 16
  how to help, 17
coastal climate, 10
coastal habitats. *See also*
  iconic birds by
    habitat
  bays and estuaries, 10–11
  coastal prairies and
    fields, 14
  forests, 13–14
  freshwater wetlands, 15
  habitat destruction, 16
  ocean, 13
  rocky shores and islands,
    11–12
  sandy beaches and dunes,
    12–13

coastal hazards, 18–19

Coastal Observation and Seabird Survey Team (COASST), 17

coastal prairies and fields as habitat, 14

Coast Range mountains, 10

Code of Birding Ethics, 20

Colaptes auratus, 191

Columbia River Estuary, East Sand Island, 165

Columbidae family, 30

Common Goldeneye, 76–77

Common Loon, 88–89

Common Merganser, 78–79

Common Murre, 8, 9, 36–37

Common Raven, 196–197

Common Yellowthroat, 15, 272–273

conservation
efforts that return land to coastal tribes, 10
helping coastal birds, 17
threats to coastal birds, 16

Cooper's Hawk, 170, 171

coots, 25, 83

cormorants, 16, 26, 98–103

Cornell Lab of Ornithology, 20

Corthylio calendula, 221

Corvidae family, 31

corvids, 31

Corvus brachyrhynchos, 195

Corvus corax, 197

crests, brightly colored, 32

crows, 31, 194–195

D

Dark-eyed Junco, 250–251

DDT, 105, 169

diurnal raptors, 29

diving birds, foraging grounds, 13

Double-crested Cormorant, 102–103

doves, 30

dowitchers, 11, 134–135

Downy Woodpecker, 186–187, 189

Dryobates pubescens, 187

Dryobates villosus, 189

ducks
characteristics, 25
fishing line entanglement, 16
foraging grounds, 13
species profiles, 52–81

Dunlin, 125, 128–129

Dusky Canada Goose, 50, 51

E

eagles, 29, 167, 176–177

Eared Grebe, 92, 93

eBird (website and app), 20

Eckman Lake, 91

egrets, 28, 146–147

Elegant Tern, 164, 165

Empidonax difficilis, 225

endangered / threatened species, 16, 41

estuarine mudflats, 11, 19

ethics, 20

Euphagus cyanocephalus, 269

Eurasian Collared-Dove, 182, 183

Eurasian Wigeon, 60, 61

European Starlings, 203

Evening Grosbeak, 284, 285

F

Falconidae family, 29

falcons, 29, 178–181

falcons vs. hawks, 29

Falco peregrinus, 181

Falco sparverius, 179

feet, shapes and functions, 25–26, 28

fence lines, 14, 257

field marks, 22, 28, 125, 175

finches, 34, 242–249

Firecrests, 32

fishing line entanglement, 16, 17

Flamecrests, 32

flycatchers, 33, 224–227

food resources. *See* coastal habitats

food web in bays and estuaries, 10–11

forests
birding tips, 14
as habitat, 13–14
iconic birds, 14
preservation of old-growth forests, 16, 17

Fox Sparrow, 260–261

Fratercula cirrhata, 45

Fringillidae family, 34

Fulica americana, 83

G

Gadwall, 56–57

Gavia immer, 89

Gavia pacifica, 87

Gavia stellata, 85

Gaviidae family, 25

gear and safety, 18–19

geese, 25, 46–51

Geothlypis trichas, 273

Glaucous Gull, 162, 163
Glaucous-winged Gull, 161, 162–163
godwits, 11, 12
Goldcrests, 32
Golden-crowned Kinglet, 215, 218–219, 221
Golden-crowned Sparrow, 254–255
Golden Eagle, 176, 177
goldeneye, common. *See* Common Goldeneye
golf courses, 49, 51, 115
gravel consumption, 30
Great Blue Heron, 144–145, 147
Great Egret, 14, 146–147
Greater Scaup, 66–67
Greater Yellowlegs, 142–143
grebes, 11, 13, 22, 26, 92–97
Green-winged Teal, 52–53
grosbeaks, 284–285
guillemots, 22
gulls, 28, 150–163

H

habitats. *See* coastal habitats; iconic birds by habitat
Haematopodidae family, 27
Haematopus bachmani, 107
Haemorhous mexicanus, 243
Haemorhous purpureus, 245
Hairy Woodpecker, 188–189
Haliaeetus leucocephalus, 177
Hammond's Flycatcher, 224, 225

Harlequin Duck, 8, 11, 68–69
hawks, 29, 167, 170–176
hawks vs. falcons, 29
Heermann's Gull, 8, 21, 150–151
Hermit Thrush, 236, 237
Hermit Warbler, 14, 278–279
herons, 15, 28, 144–145
Herring Gull, 158–159, 163
Hirundinidae family, 31
Hirundo rustica, 209
Histrionicus histrionicus, 69
"Hollywood Finches", 243
Horned Grebe, 92–93
House Finch, 242–243
House Sparrow, 203
House Wren, 228, 229
hummingbirds, 198–201
hunting adaptations, 29
Hutton's Vireo, 220, 221
Hydroprogne caspia, 165

I

Iceland Gull, 158, 159
iconic birds by habitat
  bays and estuaries, 11
  coastal prairies and fields, 14
  forests, 14
  freshwater wetlands, 15
  ocean, 13
  rocky shores and islands, 11
  sandy beaches and dunes, 12
Icteridae family, 35
Indigenous peoples as original stewards, 10
Ixoreus naevius, 235

J

jays, 31, 192–193
jetties, 11
Junco hyemalis (oreganus group), 251

K

Killdeer, 15, 114–115
kingfishers, 30, 184–185
kinglets, 14, 32, 218–222, 277

L

Lapland Longspur, 256, 257
Laridae family, 28
Larus argentatus, 158–159
Larus brachyrhynchus, 153
Larus californicus, 156–157
Larus delawarensis, 155
Larus glaucescens, 163
Larus heermanni, 151
Larus occidentalis, 161
Least Sandpiper, 15, 125, 130–131
Leiothlypis celata, 271
Lesser Goldfinch, 248, 249
Lesser Scaup, 66, 67
Lesser Yellowlegs, 142, 143
Limnodromus griseus, 135
Limosa fedoa, 119
Lincoln's Sparrow, 258, 259
Long-billed Curlew, 116, 117
Long-billed Dowitcher, 134, 135
loons, 11, 13, 22, 25, 85–90
Loxia curvirostra, 247

M

Mallard, 58–59
Marbled Godwit, 118–119

Marbled Murrelet, 13, 18, 40–41
Mareca americana, 61
Mareca strepera, 57
Marine Protected Areas, 17
Marsh Wren, 15, 230–231
Megaceryle alcyon, 185
merganser, common. *See Common Merganser*
Mergus merganser, 79
Merlin, 129, 178, 179
migration, 9
mixed-species flocks, 14, 31, 35, 221, 277
Molothrus ater, 267
mudflats, 11, 19
murrelets, 16
murres, 8, 13, 16. *See also Common Murre*

N

names of birds, 21
Nannopterum auritum, 103
nesting sites
disturbance of, 16
largest Caspian Tern colony, 165
seasonal closures and restrictions, 17
sensitivity around, 20
Northern Flicker, 190–191
Northern Harrier, 15, 170–171
Northern Pintail, 62–63
Northern Rough-winged Swallow, 202, 203
Northern Shoveler, 54–55
Numenius phaeopus, 117
nuthatches, 277

O

ocean
climate change effects, 16
as habitat, 13
iconic oceangoing birds, 13
safety, 18–19
tides, 11–12, 18–19
ocean-friendly options when eating seafood, 17
Orange-crowned Warbler, 270–271
Oregon Beach Bill, 9
Oregon Coast, 10, 18–19
Oregon Dunes Recreation Area, 9
Oregon Junco, 251
osprey, 29, 168–169
owls, 13, 170, 171
oystercatchers, 16, 27, 106–107

P

Pacific Golden-Plover, 109
Pacific Loon, 13, 86–87
Pacific-slope Flycatcher, 224–225
Pacific Wren, 14, 228–229
Pandion haliaetus, 169
Pandionidae family, 29
paralytic shellfish poisoning, 163
Paridae family, 32
parking lots, 115, 155, 159, 161, 163, 269
Parulidae family, 35
Passerculus sandwichensis, 257
Passerellidae family, 34
Patagioenas fasciata, 183
Pelagic Cormorant, 100–101

Pelecanidae family, 26
pelicans, 26, 104–105
Peregrine Falcon, 8, 20, 129, 180–181
pesticides, 105, 169, 177
Petrochelidon pyrrhonota, 211
Phalacrocoracidae family, 26
phalaropes, 137
Phalaropus lobatus, 137
Pheucticus melanocephalus, 285
phoebes, 14
Picidae family, 30
Pied-billed Grebe, 90–91
Pigeon Guillemot, 38–39
pigeons, 30, 182–183
Pipilo maculatus, 263
Piranga ludoviciana, 283
"pishing", 34
plovers, 11, 12, 17, 27, 108–115
plumage. *See individual species profiles*
Pluvialis squatarola, 109
Podiceps auritus, 93
Podiceps grisegena, 95
Podicipedidae family, 26
Podilymbus podiceps, 91
Poecile atricapillus, 212–213
Poecile rufescens, 215
Portland Audubon, 17
Procellariidae family, 28
Progne subis, 203
puffins, 13
Purple Finch, 244–245
Purple Martin, 202–203

R

rails, 25
Rallidae family, 25
raptors, 13, 15, 168–169

raptors, diurnal, 29. *See also* eagles; hawks; osprey

rarities, documenting, 18

ravens, 31, 196–197

Red-breasted Merganser, 80–81

Red Crossbill, 246–247

Red-necked Grebe, 94–95

Red-necked Phalarope, 136–137

Red Phalarope, 136, 137

Red-shouldered Hawk, 14, 172–173

Red-tailed Hawk, 174–175

Red-throated Loon, 84–85

Red-winged Blackbird, 264–265

Regulidae family, 32

Regulus satrapa, 219

Rhinoceros Auklet, 8, 42–43

Ring-billed Gull, 153, 154–155

Ring-necked Duck, 64–65

Rock Pigeon, 182, 183

Rock Sandpiper, 122, 123

rocky shores and islands as habitat, 11–12

Rough-legged Hawk, 174, 175

Ruby-crowned Kinglet, 220–221

Ruddy Turnstone, 120, 121

Rufous Hummingbird, 31, 200–201

S

safety
  ocean and coastal hazards, 18–19

  when exploring mudflats, 11

Sanderling, 12, 125, 126–127

sandpipers, 11, 27, 124–125

sandpipers and allies, species profiles, 116–143

sandy beaches and dunes as habitat, 12–13

Savannah Sparrow, 256–257

Sayornis nigricans, 226–227

Say's Phoebe, 226, 227

scaups, 67

Scolopacidae family, 27

scoters, 11, 13, 16, 22

"Seagull" as misnomer, 157

Selasphorus rufus, 201

Semipalmated Plover, 112–113, 131

Semipalmated Sandpiper, 132, 133

Setophaga coronata, 275

Setophaga occidentalis, 279

Setophaga townsendi, 277

sewage and settling ponds, 15

shearwaters, 13, 28, 148–149

shellfish poisoning, 163

shorebirds, 11, 12, 15, 27

Short-billed Dowitcher, 134–135

Short-billed Gull (formerly Mew Gull), 152–153, 155

Short-eared Owl, 170, 171

Snowy Plover, 12, 16, 17, 21

Solitary Sandpiper, 142, 143

songbirds, 13, 14, 15

Song Sparrow, 258–259

Sooty Shearwater, 28, 148–149

South Coast, 10

sparrows, 14, 34, 250–263

Spatula clypeata, 55

species, similar, 23

species abundance, 23

Spinus tristis, 249

Spotted Sandpiper, 138–139, 141

Spotted Towhee, 262–263

Steller's Jay, 21, 192–193

Surfbird, 11, 121, 122–123

Surf Scoter, 8, 70–71

Swainson's Thrush, 14, 236–237

swallows, 31, 202–211

Sylviidae family, 32

T

Tachycineta bicolor, 205

Tachycineta thalassina, 207

tanagers, 35, 282–283

terns, 28, 165–166

thrushes, 33, 234–239

Thryomanes bewickii, 233

tides, 11–12, 18–19

Townsend's Warbler, 21, 276–277, 279

Tree Swallow, 204–205

Tringa incana, 141

Trochilidae family, 31

Troglodytes pacificus, 229

Troglodytidae family, 33

tubenoses, 28

Tufted Puffin, 44–45

Turdidae family, 33

Turdus migratorius, 239

Turkey Vulture, 166–167

turnstones, 16

Tyrannidae family, 33

U

Uria aalge, 37
Urile pelagicus, 101
Urile penicillatus, 99

V

Varied Thrush, 234–235
Vaux's Swift, 202, 203
viewing gear, 13, 18
Violet-Green Swallow,
    206–207
Vireo gilvus, 223
Vireonidae family, 32–33
vireos, 32, 220–223
volunteer community
    science projects, 17
vultures, 29, 166–167

W

Wandering Tattler, 140–141
warblers, 35, 270–281
Warbling Vireo, 222–223

waterfowl, 15, 25
waxwings, 34, 240–241
Western Grebe, 96–97
Western Gull, 160–161, 163
Western Sandpiper, 125,
    132–133
Western Snowy Plover,
    110–111
Western Tanager, 282–283
wetlands as habitat, 15
Whimbrel, 12, 116–117
White-crowned Sparrow,
    252–253
White-throated Sparrow,
    254, 255
White-winged Scoter, 13, 71,
    72–73
Wilson's Warbler, 280–281
wings
    falcons, 28
    gulls and terns, 28
    hummingbirds, 31

pelicans, 26
shearwaters, 28
swallows, 31
woodpeckers, 30, 186–192
wrens, 33, 228–233
Wrentit, 32, 216–217

Y

Yellow-rumped Warbler,
    273, 274
    "Audubon's", 273, 274
    "Myrtle", 273, 274
yellowthroat, common.
    See Common
    Yellowthroat
Yellow Warbler, 270, 271,
    280, 281

Z

Zonotrichia leucophrys, 253